Übungsbuch

Compact Schülerhilfen
Englisch
Wortschatz

Julia Heller

Compact Verlag

© 1997 Compact Verlag München
Redaktion: Andrea Forster, Barry Sandoval
Umschlaggestaltung: Sabine Jantzen, Inga Koch
Illustration: Franz Gerg
Printed in Germany
ISBN 3-8174-7394-X
7373941

Inhalt

Wie du mit diesem Buch lernen kannst!	4
A. *Übungen*	**5**
1. Substantive	5
2. Pronomen	10
3. Adjektive und Adverbien	12
4. Verben	17
5. Präpositionen	24
6. Konjunktionen: *if* und *when*	28
7. Groß- und Kleinschreibung	30
8. Leicht verwechselbare Wörter	31
9. Sonstige Fehlerquellen	56
B. *Vermischte Tests*	**59**
1. Multiple Choice	59
2. Fehlertexte	70
3. Lückentexte	72
4. Übersetzungen	74
Lösungen	**79**

Wie du mit diesem Buch lernen kannst!

Die englische Sprache gut zu beherrschen gelingt dir nur, wenn du auch gute englische Wortschatzkenntnisse hast. Mit den Übungen in diesem Buch trainierst du alle wichtigen Grundsätze und Besonderheiten und gelangst bei der Anwendung des Gelernten zu mehr Sicherheit.

Im A-Teil findest du zahlreiche Einsetz- und Übersetzungsaufgaben zu den verschiedenen Wortarten und Wortformen. Im B-Teil kannst du mit Tests deine Kenntnisse überprüfen und vertiefen.

Die Übungsbücher enthalten verständlich formulierte Aufgaben in unterschiedlichem Schwierigkeitsgrad. Sie helfen dir, mögliche Fehler gezielt wegzutrainieren.

Kernpunkt der Übungsbücher sind die speziellen Übungen zu den einzelnen Themenbereichen. Deinen Lernfortschritt kannst du ganz einfach sofort kontrollieren: Bearbeite die Aufgaben Schritt für Schritt und vergleiche deine Ergebnisse mit den Lösungen am Ende des Buches!

Nun viel Erfolg!

Professor Magnus hilft dir, dich zurechtzufinden:

= Aufgabe: Alle Aufgaben solltest du schriftlich in einem gesonderten Arbeitsheft lösen.

= Testaufgabe zur Wiederholung des Gelernten

Alle Aufgabenstellungen sind rot markiert.

A. ÜBUNGEN

1. Substantive

1.1 Pluralbildung

Exercise 1: Setze die folgenden Substantive in den Plural. Beachte, dass einige von ihnen unregelmäßige Pluralformen bilden.

strawberry, journey, leaf, guy, lady, bus, buzz, kiss, hoof, quiz, issue, menu, half, fly, tooth, proof, mouse, louse, roof, canoe, wife, loaf, chief, safe

Exercise 2: Übersetze das Substantiv in Klammern, füge es in die Lücke ein und antworte dann auf die vollständige Frage im Singular.
Beispiel: *How many ... (Hunde) can you see? - dogs; I can see one dog.*

1. How many ... (Fische) are in the pond?
2. How many ... (Würfel) do you need for this game?
3. How many ... (Halstücher) did she buy yesterday?
4. How many ... (Tomaten und Kirschen) have you eaten?
5. How many ... (Echos) can you hear?
6. How many ... (Schafe) have been killed by the wolf?
7. How many ... (Wölfe) have been shot?

Exercise 3: Bilde die Singularformen der folgenden Substantive:

geese, lorries, zeros, bodies, heroes, men, pennies, volcanoes, crises, radios, axes, holidays, tornadoes, studios, selves, kangaroos, pence, mosquitoes

Exercise 4: Wie lauten folgende Sätze im Englischen?

1. Ein Sack Kartoffeln wiegt zehn Kilo.
2. Dieser Bauer hat fünf Hühner und acht Rinder (= Stück Vieh): drei Kälber, drei Kühe und zwei Ochsen.
3. „Haben Sie Kinder?" – „Ja, ich habe zwei Babys. Es sind Zwillinge."
4. Jeden Morgen müssen die Jungen sich die Zähne putzen.
5. Sei vorsichtig mit diesen Messern!
6. Acht Menschen verloren bei dem Unfall ihr Leben.
7. Er hat große Füße und sein linker Fuß ist sogar noch größer als der rechte.
8. Die neue Fernsehsendung dauert eineinhalb Stunden.

1.2 Singularbegriffe

Exercise 5: Übersetze die folgenden Sätze. Beachte, dass einige Wörter keinen Plural bilden und daher auf andere Weise zählbar gemacht werden müssen.

1. Ich versuchte ihm zu helfen, aber er will keine Ratschläge.
2. Doktor Burns gab mir einen guten Rat.
3. Es tut mir Leid, aber ich kann Ihnen keine weiteren Informationen geben.
4. Ich benötige einige Informationen.
5. Die Möbel in Fräulein Simpsons Haus sind ziemlich extravagant.
6. Ich habe mehrere Möbel für unser Wohnzimmer gekauft.
7. Mein Vater bekommt allmählich graue Haare. (= die Haare werden grau)
8. Herr Ober! In meiner Suppe ist ein Haar!
9. Ist das eine gute oder eine schlechte Nachricht?
10. Es ist nur noch ein Gepäckstück übrig.

10. Früher hat Harold jeden Abend die Nachrichten angeschaut.
12. „Wo ist Ihr Gepäck, gnädige Frau?", fragte der Portier.

1.3 Pluralbegriffe

Exercise 6: Übertrage die folgenden Sätze ins Englische:

1. Ich brauche eine neue Hose. Diese Hose ist zu groß für mich.
2. Ich kann meine Brille nicht finden. Weißt du, wo sie ist?
3. „Wie viel kostet diese Schere?" – „Zehn Dollar." – „Zehn Dollar für eine Schere?"
4. Ich bekam in allen Fächern außer Mathematik und Physik gute Noten.
5. Mein Bruder ist gestern die Treppe hinuntergefallen und hat sich eine Rippe gebrochen.
6. „Ihre Lunge ist weiß wie Schnee", sagte der Doktor lächelnd.
7. „Ihre ganze Kleidung wurde gestohlen?" – „Nein, nur ein Kleid und eine kurze Hose."

Exercise 7: Übersetze die unterstrichenen Begriffe. Achte auf die Bedeutungsunterschiede von Singular- und Pluralformen:

1. Our neighbours are strange people.
2. Our teacher is writing a book about the peoples of North America.
3. Every single piece of luggage was checked at customs.
4. I found it difficult to get used to the customs of the Japanese.
5. "Where are your manners?" complained the old lady when the policemen handcuffed her.
6. "Do it in this manner," the teacher advised me.
7. I'm not interested in politics.

8. It's not just any <u>work of art</u> – it's a masterpiece!
9. My school is right <u>behind the waterworks</u>.
10. Our new neighbours have a son who is your <u>age</u>.
11. It took me <u>ages</u> to find this house.
12. I never drink <u>spirits</u>.
13. "The most important thing is <u>team spirit</u>," said the coach.

1.4 Bezeichnungen für Länder, Nationalitäten und Sprachen

Exercise 8: Füge die passenden Länder- und Nationalitätenbezeichnungen in die Lücken ein. Ergänze wenn nötig den fehlenden Artikel:

1. ... call their country "Nippon".
2. Christopher Columbus was ...
3. The language spoken in Spain is ...
4. Most ... are fond of pizza and spaghetti.
5. The ... word for love is "amour".
6. The kilt is a traditional ... garment.
7. Berlin is the new ... capital.
8. Elvis Presley was a very famous ...
9. ... are famous for cuckoo clocks and chocolate.
10. The capital of ... is Bern.
11. Shakespeare was ... He was born in Stratford-on-Avon.
12. Before I left ..., I visited my aunt in Paris.
13. He was born in Ankara, the capital of ..., so he's of ... nationality.

Exercise 9: Übersetze die folgenden Sätze ins Englische. Überlege, ob du ein Substantiv, ein substantiviertes Adjektiv (siehe 3.1) oder ein Adjektiv verwenden musst:

1. Er ist Grieche; seine Frau ist Türkin, aber sie spricht Griechisch.
2. Zwei Griechen fragten mich, wo der Bahnhof ist.

3. Die Iren nennen ihre Insel „Eire".
4. Im Himalaya traf ich drei Schweizer und eine Spanierin.
5. Meine Tochter ist gut in Deutsch, aber in Französisch ist sie noch besser.
6. Die Vereinigten Staaten liegen (= sind) in Nordamerika.
7. Wein ist in Frankreich viel billiger als in Deutschland.
8. Letztes Jahr verbrachten sie ihren Urlaub in Österreich.
9. Warst du jemals in Australien?
10. Gibt es das Wort „Zeitgeist" im Englischen?
11. Es tut mir Leid, aber ich kann kein Japanisch, und Chinesisch kann ich auch nicht.
12. Er spricht Bayerisch; deshalb kannst du ihn nicht verstehen.
13. Er erzählte mir einen Witz über einen Engländer und einen Franzosen.

2. Pronomen

2.1 Personalpronomen

Exercise 10: Übersetze die folgenden Sätze. Denke daran, dass „es" nicht immer mit *it* wiedergegeben werden kann.

1. „Wer ist da?" – „Wir sind's, Tom und Mary!"
2. „Hast du meinen Kuchen gegessen?" – „Wer, ich?"
3. Es gibt drei Krankenhäuser in dieser Stadt.
4. Ich habe Mary gefragt, aber sie wusste es nicht.
5. Es freut mich, dass sich deine Mutter besser fühlt.
6. „Wie geht es Ihnen, Herr Jekyll?" – „Oh, danke, es geht mir gut, Herr Hyde."
7. Zieh dir Schuhe an, bevor du gehst.
8. Wenn ich er wäre, würde ich es nicht tun.
9. Schau dir den Hund da drüben an! Er jagt den Postboten!
10. „Wer sind diese Leute?" – „Das sind meine Freunde."
11. Es tut mir Leid, dass ich mich verspätet habe *(be late)*.

2.2 Indefinitpronomen

Exercise 11: Setze *some/any* bzw. *much/many* in die Lücken ein. Beachte, dass *much/many* als Objekt eines Aussagesatzes meist durch *a lot of* ersetzt wird:

1. How ... is this dress?
2. Did he eat ... cherries at all?
3. How ... cherries have been eaten?
4. "Are there ... cherries left?" – "Yes, here are ..."
5. Sorry, I haven't got ... cherries. I'm sold out.
6. There are too ... people in this lift. I'll take the stairs.
7. ... girl was asking for you yesterday.
8. Would you like ... sugar in your coffee?

9. Give me a newspaper – ... newspaper will do.
10. Does she have ... pets in her house? Yes, she's got a Siamese cat.
11. She caught ten flies in as ... minutes.
12. How ... money do you have? I haven't got ... money, but my father has got ... money.
13. Twenty people came to my party – ... stayed for hours but ... left when the rain set in.
14. Ann didn't eat ... meat. She's a vegetarian.

Exercise 12: Setze *each/every (one)* bzw. *either/neither* in die Lücken ein:

1. ... of the books is a different colour.
2. I've got two umbrellas. You can have ...
3. Congratulations! ... student passed the test!
4. Those books are three pounds ...
5. I answered both questions but unfortunately ... answer was correct.
6. There were two people in the car. ... of them was injured and had to be taken to hospital.
7. There were twenty people in the bus. ... of them was injured.
8. "Are there enough chairs for the guests?" – "There's one chair for ..."
9. I haven't told ... of my parents about the broken window.
10. "Did you choose the red one or the blue one?" – "I chose ... of them. They were too expensive."
11. ... time I meet her she has a new hairdo.
12. There's an emergency exit at ... end of the plane.
13. I'm so proud of my students! ... of them received a diploma.

3. Adjektive und Adverbien

3.1 Substantivierung des Adjektivs

Exercise 13: Überlege beim Übersetzen der folgenden Sätze, ob das jeweilige Adjektiv im Englischen allein als Substantiv stehen kann oder einen Begleiter/ein Stützwort benötigt:

1. Sie hasst alles Gelbe.
2. Ein Pessimist ist immer auf das Schlimmste gefasst *(be prepared)*.
3. Der Angeklagte weigerte sich, seine Schuld zuzugeben.
4. Die Verwundeten und die Kranken wurden ins nächstgelegene Krankenhaus gebracht.
5. „Ich nehme den Großen!", rief Jimmy und zeigte auf den riesigen Teddybären in der Ecke.
6. „Das Seltsame ist, dass die Tote in der Küche gefunden wurde", sagte Watson.
7. Robin Hood nahm Geld von den Reichen und gab es den Armen.
8. Die Toten wurden eilig begraben, weil ein Sturm aufkam.
9. Die Anwesenden bemerkten die Spinne nicht.

3.2 Steigerung des Adjektivs

Exercise 14: Bilde aus dem vorgegebenen Satz einen Satz im Superlativ.
Beispiel: *Mount Everest is a high mountain. – ... (in the world) – Mount Everest is the highest mountain in the world.*

1. He's a famous actor. – ... (in this country)
2. It was an interesting performance. – ... (of the evening)
3. This is an old house. – ... (in our town)
4. My son is a good student. – ... (in his class)
5. Tracy is a beautiful girl. – ... (I've ever seen)

6. It was a happy day. – ... (in his life)
7. You're a bad football player. – ... (I know)
8. Grandpa told us a funny story. – ... (I've ever heard)
9. Wednesday was a hot day. – ... (of the year)
10. She wore a pretty dress. – ... (she had)
11. She bought an ugly handbag. – ... (in the shop)
12. Marrying her was a stupid thing. – (he's ever done)
13. The girl stole an expensive watch. – (she could find)

> *Exercise 15:* Fülle die Lücken mit den Komparativformen der folgenden Adjektive: *sad, cheap, dry, good, hard, hungry, old, bad, wet, busy, old, long, soon, much, angry, few, early, little*

1. "Why are you crying?" – "I've never heard a ... story."
2. Do you know a ...-working man than him?
3. Linda is the ... of the two sisters. She's even ... than my brother.
4. The ... it took, the ... he became with his wife.
5. John is not very good at maths. He's got ... marks than his brother.
6. I have never met a ... man than him. He's working all the time.
7. He took ... salt but more chilli.
8. Very good, Sam! Your French is even ... than your English.
9. Those apples are ... than the pears.
10. The ... you leave, the ... you'll arrive.
11. The paint is ... on the sunny side of the fence; on the shady side it is much ...
12. The ... he ate, the ... I became.

3.3 Adjektive auf -ly

Exercise 16: Vervollständige die Satzpaare, indem du das vorgegebene Wort in Klammern im ersten Satz als Adjektiv, im zweiten als Adverb an der richtigen Stelle einfügst:

1a. Newsweek is a magazine. (weekly)
1b. This magazine is published.
2a. He's got a smile. (friendly)
2b. He smiled at me.
3a. The Millers are on their trip to Spain. (yearly)
3b. The Nobel Prize is awarded.
4a. We had lunch. (early)
4b. We had lunch.
5a. Ann's got a voice. (lovely)
5b. She sang the song.
6a. Look at that dog! (ugly)
6b. It bares its teeth.
7a. I enjoyed my visits to Grandma. (daily)
7b. I used to visit Grandma.
8a. I don't like that boy. (silly)
8b. Whenever I meet him he looks at me.

3.4 Formgleichheit von Adjektiven und Adverbien

Exercise 17: Füge das Adverb bzw. Adjektiv ein, das dem deutschen Begriff in Klammern entspricht (Tip: Jedes der gesuchten englischen Wörter kommt mindestens zweimal vor.):

1. Everyone got to the station in good time; ... (nur) Roger was ... (spät).
2. My girl-friend has got blue eyes, ... (blonde) hair and a ... (ziemlich) ... (hübsches) smile.
3. The other students treated him quite ... (fair) although he spoke ... (schlecht) of them.

4. We are ... (nahe) related but I ... (kaum) know him.
5. Have you seen my parents ... (kürzlich)?
6. Sheila is the ... (einzige) girl in our class.
7. This was a ... (höchst) amusing film.
8. Paula dresses ... (gut), but Laura dresses much ... (hübscher).
9. "Do you feel ... (gut)?" – "No, I'm afraid I'm ... (krank)."
10. Mount Whitney is 4,418 metres high. That's ... (beinahe) 14,500 feet.
11. The shop is quite ... (nahe); it's ... (gleich) around the corner.
12. The judge's verdict was hard but ... (gerecht).
13. Yesterday I received a ... (höchst) annoying letter from our landlord.
14. In summer she drinks ... (hauptsächlich, meist) water.

3.5 *still/yet/already*

Exercise 18: Füge *still, yet* oder *already* in die Lücken ein. Achte dabei auf die Satzaussage und die Position der Adverbien:

1. The doctor had ... left when I returned.
2. "Will the doctor ... be here when I get back?"– "No, he must leave at nine o'clock."
3. "Have you finished your homework?" – "No, not ..."
4. "Does your mother ... live in Islington?" – "No, she moved to Kensington two years ago."
5. I haven't read the paper ... Don't throw it away.
6. I've ... been to the Louvre. Why don't we go somewhere else today?
7. It's midnight and he's ... at work.
8. I met him only two hours ago and I ... like him.
9. He broke my heart but I ... like him.
10. By the time she had walked one mile, she was ... exhausted.
11. The letter I sent him hasn't arrived ...

Exercise 19: Übersetze nun die folgenden Sätze unter Verwendung von *still, yet* oder *already:*

1. Mary ist noch im Bett.
2. Ist es schon Mitternacht?
3. Es hat noch nicht aufgehört zu regnen.
4. Es regnet noch.
5. Wir haben noch nicht zu Abend gegessen *(have dinner)*.
6. Sie war schon da, als ihre Eltern ankamen.
7. Paul ist noch hier.
8. Paul ist noch nicht gegangen.

4. Verben

4.1 *make, do* und *take*

> *Exercise 20:* Welches der drei Verben passt in die Lücke? Setze es in der erforderlichen Form ein:

1. Catherine went upstairs to ... her homework for the next day.
2. I ... a mistake when I opened the lion's cage.
3. I'll ... this exercise for you, all right?
4. While my mother was ... the dishes, the phone rang.
5. The witness had to ... an oath to tell the truth.
6. It's hard to ... friends with the new pupil. He's very shy.
7. Our company doesn't ... much business with American companies.
8. Before she went to Tokyo, she ... an elementary course in Japanese.
9. Professor Blair's students are supposed to ... notes throughout the lecture.
10. Martin Luther King ... a famous speech on the civil rights issue in 1963.
11. Last weekend we ... a trip to Coney Island.
12. Terence ... a photo of the World Trade Center before we went to the station.
13. Yesterday we ... a lot of sport at school.
14. My parents like to ... their holidays in August.
15. Every evening Mrs Taylor ... a hot bath.
16. Watson was ... a crossword puzzle when Holmes returned.
17. The boss asked his secretary to ... a translation for him.
18. Don't ... so much noise! Your father is sleeping.
19. Most housewives ... their shopping in the morning.
20. Grandpa ... his driving test in 1947.

4.2 Reflexive Verben

Exercise 21: Übersetze die Verben in Klammern und füge sie in der passenden Form in die Lücken ein. Verwende nur englische Verben, die **kein** Reflexivpronomen bedingen.

1. I ... (sich fragen) whether Judy will arrive at the station on time. It's half past eight!
2. Look at that wrecked car! I ... (sich wundern) that nobody was injured.
3. Last week the teacher ... (sich beschweren) to my mother about my poor marks.
4. "Stop ... (sich benehmen) like a lunatic, Mr Miller!" the nurse shouted.
5. Mr Carson ... (sich verlieben) with the car at once.
6. He ... (sich ergeben) to the car dealer and signed the contract.
7. "You can ... (sich verlassen) on me to take good care of your dog," Mr Woodhouse said.
8. "Let's ... (sich treffen) at the station," George suggested.
9. He ... (sich anziehen), ... (sich kämmen) his hair and ... (sich die Zähne putzen). Then he had breakfast.
10. Many women ... (sich fürchten) of mice.

4.3 Besonderheiten bei der Bildung der Partizipien

Exercise 22: Fülle die Lücken, indem du die Verben in Klammern in die erforderliche Partizipform setzt:

1. ... (see) that it was ... (get) dark, we went back to the car.
2. How many people have been ... (kidnap) by the terrorists?
3. "What are you ... (do)?" – "I'm ... (dye) my hair."
4. I can't answer the phone. I'm ... (bathe) the baby.
5. I'm ... (fly) to New York tomorrow.

6. He ... (stop) ... (hop) about and calmed down.
7. I ... (pity) him because he was so ugly.
8. I was ... (dig) out potatoes when suddenly a rabbit ... (zig-zag) past me.
9. My father has ... (travel) the whole world.
10. You're ... (bake) a pie? That's great! I'm ... (die) for something to eat.
11. The soldier ... (fulfil) his duty to the last.
12. Will your in-laws be ... (stay) here long?
13. "What time will you be ... (come)?" Susan asked.
14. My nephew is ... (study) medicine.
15. I had my shin-bone ... (X-ray) – it isn't broken.

4.4 Unregelmäßige Verben

Exercise 23: Beantworte die folgenden Fragen mit Hilfe der Ausdrücke in Klammern.
Beispiel: *Where did John go? (London) – John went to London.*

1. And where did he come from? (Frankfort)
2. How long did it take to get to the airport? (half an hour)
3. When did he leave his wife? (seven years ago)
4. Where did you meet Judy? (at the station)
5. What did you eat – a mouse? (no, some mousse)
6. What did you buy at Harrods? (a wedding dress)
7. What did the dress cost? (a fortune)
8. What did you try to eat? (a mouse)
9. Who did the teacher speak to? (John's parents)
10. What did he tell them? (some bad news)
11. Where did Mary put her glasses? (on the desk)
12. Why did you throw away her glasses? (they were broken)
13. How many marbles did you find that day? (a dozen)
14. Did he listen to the eight o'clock news? (no, ten o'clock news)

Exercise 24: Füge das Verb in Klammern in der erforderlichen Form in die Lücke ein:

1. "Have you ... my brother?" – "Yes, I ... him an hour ago." (see)
2. "Have you ever ... champagne?" – "Yes, I ... some when I was in France." (drink)
3. "Has that dog ... the postman before?" – "Yes, it ... him last Monday." (bite)
4. "Has he ... a new novel?" – "No, he ... his last novel in 1986." (write)
5. "Has my husband ... the bill?" – "Yes, he ... it while you were talking to the manager." (pay)
6. "Have you ... a Mercedes before?" – "Yes, I ... one when I was a chauffeur." (drive)
7. "Has the water ...?" – "No, but it ... yesterday." (rise)
8. "Have you ... the key?" – "Yes, I ... it last night." (find)
9. "Have the police ... the thief?" – "Yes, they ... him on Tuesday." (catch)
10. "Have you ... the bell, Sir?" – "Yes, I ... it hours ago!" (ring)
11. "Have you ... the cat?" – "Yes, I ... it three hours ago." (feed)
12. "Have you ... a conclusion?" – "I ... one long ago, Watson." (draw)

Exercise 25: Vervollständige Lucys Brief mit Hilfe der folgenden unregelmäßigen Verben: *catch, rise, sleep, cut, fly, go, teach, be, see, drive, feel, buy, put, grow, fall, leave, take, give up, break, sew up, wake, find, tell, lie down, sell, give:*

Dear Kathy,
Lots of things have happened during the past few months. My brother Henry ... to Rome. My father ... a new job, and my mother ... smoking. She has ... her old Chrysler and ... a new car. And she has ... me how to drive, isn't that great? By the way, have I ... you about our last trip to the countryside? It ... a nightmare. Tom ... from a tree and ... his leg, I ... a cold and

Mary ... her feet on some pieces of broken glass. A farmer ... us to the nearest hospital where a doctor ... Mary's cuts. A nurse ... Tom's arm in plaster and ... my pulse. She ... me some antibiotics and I ... tired. So I ... down and ... a nap. I ... until the doctor ... me up. I ... in a hurry, looked across the room and ... – our parents! They had come to take us home. We ... and ... back to San Francisco immediately. Believe me, country life is dangerous!

Love,
Lucy

> *Exercise 26:* Setze zunächst das *simple past* des Verbs in Klammern in die Lücke ein. Bilde dann aus dem vollständigen Satz einen zweiten Satz mit dem *past participle*.
> Beispiel: *He last ... (go) to the zoo in June. – went; He hasn't gone to the zoo since June.* Oder, in umgekehrter Reihenfolge: *He ... (not go) to the zoo since June. – hasn't gone; He last went to the zoo in June.*

1. They ... (not spend) a weekend together since January.
2. They last ... (hold) a meeting one month ago.
3. I ... (not drive) to Scotland for three years.
4. You last ... (bring) me flowers on our wedding day.
5. Tom last ... (feed) the cat two days ago!
6. Jerry ... (not sleep) on a water-bed since he was a bachelor.
7. The children last ... (swim) in the ocean four weeks ago.
8. The cleaning woman last ... (sweep) the floor on Friday.
9. The poacher last ... (shoot) a rabbit in May.
10. I ... (not ring) him up since the day I met you.
11. I last ... (wear) these glasses in 1966.
12. I ... (not wind) this watch since Wednesday.
13. I last ... (build) a sand-castle when I was five years old.
14. She last ... (sing) this aria when she was a teenager.
15. My wife ... (not buy) a new dress since spring.
16. I last ... (drink) coffee two weeks ago.
17. The car last ... (break down) two months ago.

Exercise 27: Wie lautet das *simple past* der entsprechenden englischen Verben?

1. Kathy ... (reiten) every day until the day she ... (fallen) off her horse and ... (brechen) her leg.
2. I ... (werfen) the cheddar away because it ... (riechen) odd.
3. The curtain ... (aufgehen, sich heben) and the actors ... (beginnen) their performance.
4. Mr Blair ... (schließen) his shop at 6 o'clock.
5. The dog ... (verstecken) Mr Armstrong's key under the carpet.
6. That's Mr Gomez. He ... (lehren) me mathematics.
7. She ... (verzeihen) him a long time ago.
8. They ... (übertragen) the President's speech on all channels.
9. He ... (stehen) at the bus stop and ... (lesen) a magazine.
10. He ... (herausnehmen) a cigarette and ... (anzünden) it.
11. The stranger ... (halten) out his hand and I ... (schütteln) it.
12. My grandfather ... (sich fühlen) very comfortable in that chair.
13. "The burglar ... (tragen) gloves?" – "Well, I ... (denken) so."
14. They ... (sprechen) about the election results.
15. The teacher ... (herausreißen) the first page of the book.
16. I wonder why the boy ... (tragen) so much money with him.
17. She ... (verletzen) herself when she tried to open the tin.

Exercise 28: Füge die Verben in Klammern in der erforderlichen Form *(simple past* bzw. *past participle)* ein:

1. He ... (stick) a label on the box.
2. The men ... (sit) with their heads ... (bend).
3. Have they ... (choose) their partners?
4. I ... (not know) that you ... (know) the author. How long ... (you know) him?

5. The burglar ... (flee) when the alarm ... (sound).
6. The moon ... (shine) through the window.
7. The news of Linda's accident has ... (spoil) my day.
8. The clock has just ... (strike) five.
9. When he ... (brake), the pedal ... (break) off.
10. The witness ... (swear) that he had never ... (see) the man before.
11. The teacher ... (wring) his hands in despair.
12. The love letter ... (bear) my husband's signature.
13. Her son was ... (bear) on August 10th.
14. Be careful, Mr James, this gun is ... (load)!
15. The tree is ... (load) with apples.
16. He ... (hang) his coat on a hook.
17. The man was ... (hang) for stabbing his wife with a knife.
18. When the door ... (swing) open Watson ... (spin) around.
19. The suitcase Fred ... (buy) has been ... (steal).

5. Präpositionen

5.1 Partizip/Adjektiv + Präposition

Exercise 29: Fülle die Lücken mit den passenden Präpositionen:

1. Those shoes are different ... the ones I bought.
2. This behaviour is typical ... all birds of prey.
3. My sister is good ... walking on her hands.
4. I was deeply impressed ... her beauty.
5. The two results were obtained independent ... each other.
6. I'm not interested ... your stories anymore.
7. Most students in our new class were kind ... us.
8. Before my grandmother met my grandfather, she was married ... an Irishman.
9. Many women are afraid ... going out alone at night.
10. The teacher is angry ... your cheeky answers.
11. While we were sailing along the coast, we were surprised ... a storm.
12. Don't be angry ... me! I promise I won't do it again.
13. You're very bad ... lying – why don't you tell us the truth?
14. The burglar was surprised ... the police while he was trying to open the door.
15. The teacher was surprised ... finding the room empty.

Exercise 30: Übersetze die Ausdrücke in Klammern und vervollständige damit die Sätze. Beachte die unterschiedliche Verwendung englischer und deutscher Präpositionen:

1. Carol was really ... his proposal. (überrascht von)
2. My son is very ... physics. (schlecht in)
3. Soccer is very ... American football. (anders als)
4. I'm ... the result of my exam. (enttäuscht von)
5. You look unhappy. What's ... you? (los mit)
6. Joan is very ... maths. (gut in)
7. The teacher was ... my painting. (beeindruckt von)

8. Mary ... spiders. (hat Angst vor)
9. Paula is ... joining our team. (interessiert an)
10. The nurse was very ... me. (nett zu)
11. Carol is ... a congressman. (verheiratet mit)
12. He was very ... that. (überrascht von)
13. It's ... you to forget the key. (typisch für)
14. Why didn't she say hello? Is she ... me? (böse auf)
15. My mother was very ... the broken window. (verärgert über)

5.2 Verb + Präposition

Exercise 31: Übersetze das Verb in Klammern und füge es in der richtigen Form und mit der erforderlichen Präposition in die Lücke ein:

1. I bought this picture because it ... me ... my childhood. (erinnern an)
2. My mother is ... the baby while I'm away. (kümmern um)
3. He ... Doctor Taylor's suggestion and went to hospital. (zustimmen)
4. My grandfather doesn't ... progress. (glauben an)
5. All my brother ever ... are cars. (denken an)
6. The success of a new product ... its appeal. (abhängen von)
7. When I was young I ... becoming an astronaut. (träumen von)
8. Tom ... driving me home although he was in a hurry. (bestehen auf)
9. "You never ... what I say," his wife complained. (zuhören)
10. When I told him what had happened, he ... me in surprise. (ansehen)
11. I accepted his opinion, but I didn't ... it. (übereinstimmen mit)
12. How much did you ... your new car? (zahlen für)
13. Stanley ... me ... feed the dogs. (erinnern an)
14. My father never ... me when I'm late. (anschreien)

15. We left London in the morning and ... Oxford at noon. (ankommen in)
16. Even the doctor ... my funny story. (lächeln über)
17. "Do you ... toothache?" Doctor Taylor asked. (leiden unter)
18. All the students ... the discussion. (teilnehmen an)
19. Grandfather is always ... his spectacles. (suchen nach)
20. Doctor Taylor ... his error. (sich entschuldigen für)
21. The doctor ... me ... my good health. (gratulieren zu)

Exercise 32: Wie lauten die fehlenden Präpositionen?

1. Last night I dreamt ... a blue frog with two heads.
2. All passengers arrived safely ... Moscow.
3. Mary agreed ... me that it was too cold to go for a swim.
4. I'm looking ... my little sister. Have you seen her?
5. I told him what I thought ... his letter.
6. Grandmother asked me to look ... her flowers.
7. The jury believed ... his innocence and found him not guilty.
8. Eleven countries will be taking part ... the song contest.
9. Helen had run out of money, so I had to pay ... the goods.
10. His whole future depended ... the jury's verdict.
11. The children listened breathlessly ... Grandfather's story.
12. Stanley never apologizes ... coming home late.
13. The teacher smiled ... me and said "Well done, Paul!"
14. "What's wrong ... Mr Barks?" – "He's still suffering ... the accident he had last winter."
15. "I always have to remind you ... brush your teeth," my mother said angrily.
16. The doctor insisted ... checking my blood pressure.
17. Mr and Mrs Barks are always shouting ... each other.
18. This dog reminds me ... the one we used to have back in England.
19. I congratulated myself ... having done the right thing.
20. He looked ... himself in the mirror and detected a green spot on his cheek.
21. The client didn't agree ... my conditions, so I refused to help him.

5.3 Präposition + Substantiv/Pronomen

Exercise 33: *by, at, on, in* – welche Präposition passt in die Lücke?

1. My daughter Ann is a student ... New York University.
2. Let's go to the lake ... bike – it's much more fun!
3. The hero dies ... the end of the story.
4. Burt, there's a picture of you ... the paper!
5. Billiards isn't often ... TV.
6. How is your son getting on ... school?
7. It's quite exciting to live ... a city like New York.
8. You're never ... time! Don't you have a watch?
9. I was listening to a Beatles special ... the radio when the phone rang.
10. We travelled to Houston ... plane.
11. I didn't see Tom ... the party on Wednesday.
12. This week they are showing a great film ... the cinema.
13. ... this picture you can see my whole family.
14. He retired last year and went to live ... the country.
15. When I was in Boston I saw a play ... the theatre.
16. Have you ever read a novel ... William Faulkner?
17. Why don't we go ... car?

Exercise 34: Übersetze die folgenden Sätze ins Englische:

1. Ich hoffe, der Zug wird pünktlich ankommen.
2. Meine Kinder sind den ganzen Vormittag in der Schule.
3. „Romeo und Julia" ist ein Stück von Shakespeare.
4. Ich habe das Spiel letzten Freitag im Fernsehen gesehen.
5. Wir haben das Wochenende auf dem Land verbracht.
6. Meine Mutter ist nicht zu Hause. Sie ist im Theater.
7. Gestern Abend habe ich Janet in der Stadt getroffen.
8. Mein Auto ist das blaue am Ende der Straße.
9. Dorothy fährt mit dem Bus nach Islington.
10. Hast du über den Unfall in der Zeitung gelesen?

11. Meine Schwester studiert an der Universität Biologie.
12. Ich habe die Neuigkeit im Radio gehört.
13. Gestern Abend war ich im Kino.
14. Meine Kinder fahren mit dem Rad zur Schule.
15. Wir können mit dem Zug nach Bristol fahren.
16. Auf der Party waren viele Leute.
17. Wer ist das andere Mädchen auf dem Bild?

6. Konjunktionen: if und when

Exercise 35: Übersetze die folgenden wenn-Sätze ins Englische. Entscheide jeweils, ob „wenn" mit *if* oder mit *when* wiedergegeben werden muss:

1. Wenn er das Buch gelesen hat, kann ich es haben.
2. Wenn man Eis erwärmt, schmilzt es.
3. Du kannst meinen Regenschirm nehmen, wenn du willst.
4. Wenn es heiß ist, sind die Strände überfüllt.
5. Der Lehrer wird verärgert sein, wenn ich zu spät komme.
6. Wenn der Regen aufhört, gehe ich in den Zoo.
7. Wenn ich ein Lineal hätte, würde ich es dir leihen.
8. Hast du etwas dagegen, wenn ich deinen Regenschirm nehme?
9. Ich werde John fragen, wenn ich von der Schule nach Hause komme.
10. Wenn ich du wäre, würde ich mich nicht dafür entschuldigen.

Exercise 36: Setze *when* oder *if* in die Lücken ein:

1. It was raining ... I arrived at the station.
2. My parents will be very happy ... I pass the examination.
3. Janet might phone tomorrow. ... she does, can you tell her I'm in Newcastle?
4. He was brushing his teeth ... the phone rang.

5. I think you'll pass the examination. I'll be very surprised ... you don't.
6. ... you're looking for your father you'll find him in the garden.
7. ... she had taken my advice she wouldn't be unhappy now.
8. How can he buy a new car ... he hasn't got a job?
9. ... I found the knife I knew what had happened.
10. I'm going to Boston for a week. I'll phone you ... I get back.
11. ... I found the key I would open the door.
12. ... she found the key she opened the door.
13. I'm visiting Grandma this afternoon. ... I see her, I'll tell her about your plans.
14. I might visit Grandma this afternoon. ... I see her, I'll tell her about your plans.

7. Groß- und Kleinschreibung

Exercise 37: Schreibe die folgenden Sätze ab und verbessere dabei alle Fehler:

1. paul whistler is a doctor.
2. he is doctor paul whistler.
3. god spoke to moses.
4. apollo was the greek god of music.
5. is he a minister?
6. he is the prime minister.
7. her majesty the queen gave a speech on friday.
8. elizabeth II was crowned queen in 1953 at westminster abbey.
9. oh, i love christmas pudding!
10. what's the name of this street? is it baker street?
11. your aunt bought a german car last august. who, aunt judy?
12. is sir andrew a member of the church of england?
13. penguins live at the south pole.
14. starlings fly south for winter.
15. two members of the labour party came to my birthday party.

Exercise 38: Auch hier sollst du die Rechtschreibfehler verbessern:

1. Reverend Adams Told Us To Sing The Lord's Prayer.
2. My Uncle's Car Is A Ford.
3. My Grandfather Lost His Life In The Second World War.
4. Mary Went To A Cinema At Washington Square To See "The Silence Of The Lambs".
5. The President Of The United States Received Three Members Of Parliament At The White House.
6. The President Of Our Committee Lives In A White House.

8. Leicht verwechselbare Wörter

8.1 *False Friends*

Exercise 39: Übersetze die unterstrichenen Begriffe ins Deutsche:

1. The driver <u>was lucky</u> to survive that accident.
2. <u>The actual reason</u> was that I had no money.
3. His remark and <u>the consequent laughter</u> interrupted the discussion.
4. Slow down! You're driving too <u>fast</u>!
5. Something in this dustbin smells <u>foul</u>.
6. The <u>gross income</u> has risen considerably.
7. I'm not hungry. I've just eaten a big <u>bowl</u> of salad.
8. I saw Janet and I <u>also</u> saw her new boyfriend.
9. He's too <u>self-conscious</u>; he never talks to strangers.
10. The new student was given <u>a genial welcome</u>.
11. He wrote his name on <u>a blank sheet of paper</u>.
12. It was very <u>sensible</u> of you to call the doctor.

Exercise 40: Übersetze die folgenden Sätze ins Englische. Achte besonders auf die korrekte Wiedergabe der unterstrichenen Wörter:

1. Janet war <u>glücklich</u> mit ihrem neuen Auto.
2. Miniröcke sind immer <u>aktuell</u>.
3. Ihr Sohn ist ein sehr <u>sensibles</u> Kind.
4. Er ist sehr <u>konsequent</u>: Er isst weder Fleisch noch Eier.
5. Ich bin <u>fast</u> fünf Jahre alt.
6. Wir leben in einem <u>großen</u> Haus.
7. Die <u>Bowle</u> wurde in einer Schüssel serviert.
8. Roger war krank, <u>also</u> blieb er zu Hause.
9. Martin ist <u>selbstbewusster</u> als sein Bruder.
10. Mein Großvater war ein <u>genialer</u> Wissenschaftler.
11. Er <u>putzte</u> seine Schuhe <u>blank</u>, bevor er ging.
12. Sei nicht so <u>faul</u>!

Exercise 41: Übersetze die unterstrichenen Ausdrücke ins Deutsche:

1. She's a bit <u>plump</u> but she doesn't care.
2. My father had been coughing all the time. <u>Eventually</u> he gave up smoking.
3. Pablo Picasso was a <u>famous artist</u>.
4. John felt <u>guilty</u> about the broken window.
5. The teacher was very <u>sympathetic</u> when I told him about Mary's accident.
6. <u>Be brave!</u> I'm sure the dentist won't hurt you.
7. Doctor Taylor, <u>can you spare me a few minutes</u>?
8. The doctor locked the door, <u>winked at me</u> and lit a cigarette.
9. The two girls <u>became</u> friends.
10. They <u>spend</u> a lot of time together.
11. He <u>turned around</u> and picked up the ball.

Exercise 42: Wie lauten die folgenden Sätze im Deutschen? Achte wieder besonders auf die unterstrichenen Wörter:

1. Unsere neuen Nachbarn sind ziemlich <u>sympathisch,</u> findest du nicht?
2. <u>Eventuell</u> schauen Susan und Roger heute Abend vorbei *(drop in)*.
3. Das ist eine <u>famose</u> Idee!
4. Es tut mir Leid, aber Ihr Fahrschein ist nicht mehr <u>gültig</u>.
5. Henry und Martha waren <u>brave</u> Kinder.
6. Das Mädchen <u>winkte</u>, als ihre Freunde den Raum betraten.
7. Der Gewinner <u>spendete</u> das Geld Greenpeace.
8. Dieses Gemälde ist eine <u>plumpe</u> Fälschung *(forgery)*.
9. Mein Bruder <u>spart</u> auf *(for)* ein neues Auto.
10. Roger ist sehr gut im <u>Turnen</u>.
11. Er <u>bekam</u> einen Brief von seiner Freundin.

Exercise 43: Was ist die deutsche Bedeutung der unterstrichenen Begriffe?

1. The stewardess told us to <u>fasten</u> our seat-belts.
2. Michael <u>enrolled</u> in an English course.
3. The two girls <u>wandered the woods</u> aimlessly.
4. Yesterday <u>I slept in</u> but today I'm still tired.
5. After the confession the priest <u>absolved him</u> of his sins.
6. <u>I wish</u> you all the luck in the world.
7. <u>The cost</u> of building this house was much higher than I had expected.
8. The <u>dome</u> of this cathedral was built in 1785.
9. Most <u>easels</u> are made of wood.
10. Holmes found the <u>woollen fabric</u> in the garden.
11. You should handle this chainsaw with <u>caution</u>.
12. The farmer gave me <u>this puppy</u> as a present.
13. The <u>chef</u> at this restaurant is very good.

Exercise 44: Übersetze ins Englische und achte besonders auf die unterstrichenen Begriffe:

1. Hör auf, mit deinen <u>Puppen</u> zu spielen!
2. Der <u>Igel</u> <u>rollte sich ein</u> und <u>schlief ein</u>.
3. Er <u>absolvierte</u> den Kurs in weniger als zwei Monaten.
4. Sie <u>wischte</u> sich die Tränen weg und versuchte zu lächeln.
5. Viele Christen <u>fasten</u>, um sich auf das Osterfest vorzubereiten.
6. Kannst du auf einem <u>Esel</u> reiten?
7. Viele Männer in unserer Nachbarschaft arbeiten in der <u>Fabrik</u>.
8. Er hat die <u>Kaution</u> nicht bezahlt, also habe ich das Appartement an jemand anderen vermietet *(let)*.
9. Gestern hat der <u>Chef</u> Herrn Barks gefeuert *(fire)*.
10. Der Kölner <u>Dom</u> ist ein imposantes Bauwerk.
11. <u>Wandern</u> ist weniger gefährlich als Bergsteigen.

Exercise 45: Übersetze die unterstrichenen Ausdrücke:

1. My grandmother grows <u>beans</u> in her garden.
2. The children hid in a <u>hut</u> at the lake.
3. She bought a pair of black <u>boots</u> for her sister.
4. What do you know about the <u>art</u> of cooking?
5. Mary sat <u>on the floor</u> and played with her dolls.
6. We don't accept girls in our <u>gang</u>.
7. Could you give me a <u>receipt</u> for these books?
8. I had <u>shellfish</u> for dinner and now I feel sick.
9. Let's buy a <u>gift</u> to give to Kathy.
10. The injured man was taken to hospital in an <u>ambulance</u>.
11. You can't play baseball in this <u>gymnasium</u>!
12. What a funny mug! It's got two <u>handles</u>!
13. The <u>eagle</u> is a bird of prey.

Exercise 46: Wie lauten folgende Sätze im Englischen?

1. Er setzte seinen <u>Hut</u> auf und nahm seinen Regenschirm.
2. <u>Igel</u> sind lustig anzuschauen; sie anzufassen ist weniger lustig.
3. Auf dem Fluss waren viele <u>Boote</u>.
4. Lass uns gehen! Ich mag diese <u>Art</u> Party nicht.
5. Herrn Barks Büro ist am Ende des <u>Ganges</u>.
6. In seinem Netz waren einige <u>Schellfische</u>.
7. „Wer tat das <u>Gift</u> in Frau Hathaways Tee?", fragte sich Holmes.
8. Die <u>Ambulanz</u> war überfüllt, <u>also</u> musste ich zwei Stunden warten.
9. <u>Bienen</u> sind sehr intelligente Insekten.
10. Was ist dein <u>Rezept</u> für diesen köstlichen Kuchen?
11. Der alte Mann öffnete die Türe und stellte seinen Koffer in den <u>Flur</u>.
12. Unser Sohn besuchte ein deutsches <u>Gymnasium</u>.
13. Der <u>Handel</u> mit Kaffee hat in letzter Zeit zugenommen.

Exercise 47: Übersetze die unterstrichenen Wörter:

1. The teacher told my mother that I hadn't done my <u>homework</u>.
2. He ordered two <u>lagers</u> and a sandwich.
3. The <u>undertaker</u> was very <u>sympathetic</u> toward the widow.
4. Professor Armstrong gave a <u>lecture</u> on English poetry.
5. We've lost our way. Let's have a look at the <u>map</u>.
6. I can't use the garden <u>hose</u>; it leaks.
7. Your dog has eaten all my <u>biscuits</u>!
8. I don't have enough <u>mince</u> for this recipe.
9. One <u>building</u> was destroyed by the fire.
10. Through the <u>mist</u> Holmes could see the shape of a man in the distance.
11. When the police arrived the <u>warehouse</u> was empty.
12. "I know who committed the <u>murder</u>!" Watson exclaimed.
13. The policeman showed the witnesses a <u>photograph</u> of the suspect.

Exercise 48: Achte beim Übersetzen folgender Sätze besonders auf die unterstrichenen Wörter:

1. Der <u>Mörder</u> versteckte sich in einer Höhle.
2. Wir bewahren *(keep)* unsere Waren in einem <u>Lager</u> auf.
3. Mein Sohn ist der jüngste <u>Unternehmer</u> Deutschlands.
4. „Jetzt versuche zu lächeln", sagte der <u>Fotograf</u>.
5. Was hat er dir als <u>Lektüre</u> empfohlen?
6. Mir sind kleine Boutiquen lieber *(prefer)* als <u>Warenhäuser</u>.
7. Die Sekretärin legte das Formular in eine <u>Mappe</u>.
8. Ich kann diese <u>Hose</u> nicht tragen. Sie ist schmutzig.
9. Sein Mangel an <u>Bildung</u> ist schockierend.
10. Hast du deiner Mutter bei der <u>Hausarbeit</u> geholfen?
11. <u>Mist</u> ist ein guter Dünger *(fertilizer)*.
12. Dieser Cocktail wird mit einem Blatt <u>Minze</u> serviert.
13. Das ist der beste <u>Biskuit</u>kuchen, den ich je gegessen habe!

Exercise 49: Wie lauten die unterstrichenen Ausdrücke im Deutschen?

1. Marvin is the old-timer in our group.
2. After ten years of hard work he was given a promotion.
3. The servant put some more coal on the fire.
4. The prospect of losing money made him very angry.
5. I don't like the taste of this meat.
6. The frog caught a fly with its long tongue.
7. The two tramps were looking for work.
8. He killed the snake with a stone.
9. If you do your homework at this rate you'll never finish it in time!
10. This phrasal verb has two different meanings.
11. I'm two months behind with the rent.
12. Etiquette didn't allow to criticise the Queen.
13. Who's the sender of this parcel?

Exercise 50: Übersetze die Sätze ins Englische:

1. Meine Kinder essen nie Kohl.
2. Ich verlasse mich nicht auf Reiseprospekte.
3. Wie viele Tasten hat ein Klavier?
4. Die Schnecken haben meinen Kohl gefressen!
5. Meiner Meinung nach hat Doktor Taylor Unrecht.
6. Ich habe viel Geld für diesen Oldtimer bezahlt.
7. Ich kann dir dieses Spielzeug nicht kaufen; meine Rente ist zu knapp *(small)*.
8. Was ist in dieser Flasche? Sie hat kein Etikett.
9. Ihre Eltern waren stolz, als sie ihre Promotion erhielt.
10. Der Radiosender übertrug die Rede des Präsidenten.
11. Ich habe die monatliche Rate für mein Auto immer noch nicht bezahlt.
12. Auf unserem Weg nach Detroit haben wir einen Tramper mitgenommen *(pick up)*.
13. Unser Flug wurde annulliert *(cancel)*.

8.2 Homonyme

Exercise 51: Übersetze die unterstrichenen Ausdrücke. Denke daran, dass die englischen Begriffe verschiedene Bedeutungen haben können, die sich aus dem Zusammenhang ergeben:

1. Mary tried <u>to light a candle</u> but the matches were wet.
2. At midnight Cinderella left the <u>ball</u> in a hurry.
3. The old lady <u>had a kind</u> face and a soft voice.
4. Bark beetles nest under the <u>bark</u> of certain trees.
5. "Who put that <u>spell</u> on you?" the beautiful princess asked the ugly frog.
6. The moving company packed our belongings into <u>boxes</u>.
7. All his <u>cases</u> were checked at customs.
8. On top of the hill you have <u>a fine view of Rome</u>.
9. The old lady told the thief that she had all her money <u>in the bank</u>.
10. "This is <u>a clear case</u> of suicide," Watson insisted.
11. A female fox is <u>called</u> a vixen.
12. After the <u>match</u> the coach congratulated us on our performance.
13. "There's someone at the door! <u>Blow out the candle</u>, Watson!" Holmes whispered.
14. There were 32 people <u>present</u> at our annual gathering.
15. Mr Fowler doesn't <u>like</u> his mother-in-law.
16. Holmes had to find her before the murderer did; it was <u>a race against time</u>.

Exercise 52: Hier kommen bestimmte Wörter aus Übung 51 in einer völlig anderen Bedeutung vor. Achte darauf, wenn du die unterstrichenen Passagen übersetzt:

1. <u>What kind of fruit</u> do you grow in your garden?
2. Mr Fowler listened to some <u>light music</u>.

3. "This <u>case</u> is more difficult than I thought," Holmes muttered.
4. Did your father <u>box</u> against the heavyweight champion?
5. If you don't pay the <u>fine</u> your car will be towed away.
6. Most dogs <u>bark</u> when the doorbell rings.
7. <u>How do you spell that word</u>, with a C or with an S?
8. The <u>ball</u> rolled down the street and the dog ran after it.
9. Your dog <u>looks a bit like</u> Lassie.
10. He <u>cleared away</u> the empty glasses before he left.
11. The red shoes <u>don't match</u> your yellow dress.
12. The old lady <u>dealt him a blow</u> with her handbag.
13. My father always hides our Christmas <u>presents</u> in the attic.
14. She stood on <u>the bank of the river</u> and watched the boats.
15. Is <u>the human race</u> superior to any other species?
16. When she heard the sound of breaking glass, <u>she called the police</u>.

Exercise 53: In den beiden folgenden Übungen geht es wieder um die eben geübten Homonyme. Denke beim Übersetzen der Sätze daran.

1. Der arme Roger war der Einzige ohne Tanzpartnerin *(partner)* auf dem Ball.
2. Ich habe ein Buch mit Zaubersprüchen auf unserem Speicher gefunden.
3. Er schnitzte ihren Namen in die Rinde.
4. Ich habe das Bußgeld nicht bezahlt.
5. Er steckte eine Schachtel Streichhölzer in seine Tasche.
6. Er gewann das Rennen auf einem Pferd namens „Lucky Star".
7. Ich mag diese Art Fragen nicht.
8. Der Mann setzte sich und zündete sich eine Zigarette an.
9. Holmes löste den Fall innerhalb von zwei Tagen.
10. Die Ufer des Flusses waren ölverschmutzt.
11. Alle Anwesenden applaudierten dem Sprecher.
12. Blasen Sie den Staub von diesem Stuhl, bevor Sie sich hinsetzen.
13. Ihr Hut und ihre Schuhe passten wunderbar zusammen.

Exercise 54: Wie lauten folgende Sätze im Englischen?

1. Der Lehrer bat uns, unsere Namen zu buchstabieren.
2. Du räumst den Tisch ab, ist das klar?
3. Ein Mädchen wie Alice ist schwer zu überzeugen.
4. Als der Postbote klingelte, fing der Hund an zu bellen.
5. Das Wetter war schön, also machten sie einen Spaziergang.
6. Als Jugendlicher *(teenager)* habe ich geboxt.
7. Frau Turner rief die Kinder, als es Zeit zum Abendessen war.
8. Die zwei Tiere sehen verschieden aus, gehören aber derselben Rasse an.
9. Gestern wurde die Bank ausgeraubt.
10. Herr Turner kaufte ein Geschenk für seine Frau.
11. Der Polizist war sehr freundlich und höflich.
12. Er nahm *(have)* eine leichte Mahlzeit zu sich; dann ging er zu Bett.
13. Der Dieb warf die Dollarscheine in einen Koffer.
14. Der Torwart fing den Ball mit einer Hand.
15. Watson erhielt einen Schlag auf den Kopf.
16. Das Tennisspiel dauerte vier Stunden.

8.3 Homophone

Exercise 55: Finde die passenden englischen Homophone, die die Sätze sinnvoll ergänzen. Pro Satzpaar (a + b) wird stets ein Homophonpaar (z. B. *four - fore*) gesucht. Wie lauten die zwei homophonen Begriffe im Deutschen?

1a. He ... who had written the letter.
1b. There's a ... pupil in our class.
2a. He decided to ... his children to be careful.
2b. Mrs Taylor has ... that dress several times.
3a. He didn't feel any ... in his shoulder.
3b. The burglar smashed the ... with his fist.

4a. The coach ... the ball to me.
4b. This path leads ... a forest.
5a. Which ... did the woman go?
5b. Together Judy and Laura ... 60 kilos.
6a. This shuttle bus drives back and ... between the station and the airport.
6b. On her ... birthday Judy got a red bicycle.
7a. One hour later, the water had risen to his ...
7b. Stop searching those drawers, Watson, it's a ... of time!

Exercise 56: Finde auch hier wieder die passenden englischen Homophonpaare und übersetze sie dann ins Deutsche:

1a. "Do you ... this gentleman?" Holmes asked.
1b. Don't open this door, ... matter what happens.
2a. I never ... sunglasses.
2b. I don't know ... I put my glasses.
3a. He ... a lot about me.
3b. Don't stick your ... into my affairs!
4a. Don't ... that vase! It's a present from Grandfather!
4b. The motorcyclist had to ... when a ball rolled onto the road.
5a. The coach told us to play ...
5b. The bus ... to Bath is twenty pounds.
6a. Last time your dog ... all my biscuits.
6b. There were ... children in the bath-tub!
7a. You'll have to ... until the end of the lesson.
7b. Holmes was surprised at the ... of the suitcase.

Exercise 57: Welche Homophone gehören in die Lücken? Was ist ihre deutsche Bedeutung?

1a. My father stores a lot of wine in his ...
1b. The ... of this product is a supermarket chain.
2a. Grandmother's wedding ring is very ... to me.
2b. The wooded regions of North America are full of ...

3a. "Your wife has got a ... heart," Doctor Taylor said with a frown.
3b. Saturday is my favourite day of the ...
4a. "Do you ... me?" Watson shouted through a hole in the wall.
4b. The Simpsons have lived ... for ten years.
5a. She looked up and ... a spider on the ceiling.
5b. The concert was cancelled because the singer had a ... throat.
6a. Ginger and Fred were a happy ...
6b. The neighbour threw the rotten ... back over our fence.
7a. Your're ... young to drive a car.
7b. The ... men looked at each other.
7c. What did he say ... you?

Exercise 58: Fülle die Lücken mit den geeigneten Homophonpaaren und gib deren deutsche Bedeutung an:

1a. She wore her long ... in plaits.
1b. After it had eaten the carrot, the ... licked its paws carefully.
2a. He enjoyed the ... and the fresh morning air.
2b. He wrote his name on a ... of paper.
3a. Is this the ... way to the lake?
3b. ... the answer on the blackboard!
4a. Who plays the ... of the fool?
4b. He cut the ... into halves with a sharp knife.
5a. I wonder why the cut on your face doesn't ...
5b. The ... of my left shoe is loose.
6a. Watson peered through a ... in the wall.
6b. Holmes thought the ... thing over.
7a. The captain decided to ... into the harbour.
7b. Our neighbour's house is for ...
8a. My grandfather left Germany during the ...
8b. The burglar ... gloves – he didn't leave any fingerprints.

Exercise 59: Welche englischen Homophone passen in die Lücken und wie lauten sie auf Deutsch?

1a. Our team has ... the championship!
1b. ... of those present is a murderer, Watson.
2a. "Today I will show you how to tie a ...," the teacher said.
2b. "That's ... my doll!" Tracy cried.
3a. Vegetarians don't eat ...
3b. I'd like you to ... my friend Tracy.
4a. It's a crime to ... other people's things.
4b. The stuntman had nerves of ...
5a. Roger is ... only child.
5b. ... very proud of their son.
5c. The Turners' house is over ...
6a. He picked up the frogs and put them in a ...
6b. Watson turned ... at the sight of the dead body.
7a. Have you ever ... "Oliver Twist" at school?
7b. The teacher turned ... in the face with anger.

Exercise 60: Finde die passenden Homophonpaare und übersetze sie ins Deutsche:

1a. The turkey is served with cranberry ...
1b. The ... of the reporter's information was a politician.
2a. ... your favourite pop star?
2b. Holmes wondered ... gun it was.
3a. Dan can jump ... than I can.
3b. Why don't you ... a car? It's much cheaper than going there by train.
4a. Kathy served some strawberries for ...
4b. If you ... me, I'll tell the whole story to the police!
5a. Today the ... is changing every hour.
5b. The teacher asked me ... I knew the answer.
6a. George hasn't ... the exam yet.
6b. Hurry up, it's half ... eight!
7a. Cain was the first ... of Adam and Eve.
7b. The earth orbits around the ...

Exercise 61: In jedem Satz ist (mindestens) eines der in den Übungen 55-60 behandelten Homophone versteckt – es geht also jetzt darum, das richtige Homophon bzw. die richtige Schreibweise zu finden. Übersetze den gesamten Satz ins Englische und unterstreiche dann alle darin enthaltenen Homophone:

1. Wo ist meine Brille?
2. Die Maus verschwand in einem Loch.
3. Wie ist das Wetter heute?
4. „Ich habe eine Murmel *(marble)* gefunden!" – „Hier ist noch eine!"
5. Unser neues Sofa ist sehr bequem.
6. Du kannst das Messer nicht verbiegen – es ist aus Stahl.
7. Ich weiß, dass sie dieses Kleid schon einmal getragen hat.
8. Ich bin an Ihrem Angebot nicht interessiert.
9. Tante Sylvie ist die Schwester meiner Mutter.
10. Wir verließen die Feier um halb neun.
11. Weißt du, wo er herkommt?
12. Die Luft war so kalt, dass seine Nase rot wurde.
13. Ihr blasses Gesicht errötete vor Verlegenheit.
14. Drei Tage waren seit dem ersten Verbrechen vergangen.

Exercise 62: Auch hier sollst du den gesamten Satz ins Englische übertragen und die gefundenen Homophone unterstreichen:

1. Nach zwei Wochen im Gefängnis gestand der Verdächtige alles.
2. Hat sie genug Salz in die Soße getan?
3. Mein Vater war streng, aber gerecht.
4. Wer ist der berühmteste Popstar?
5. Ich sagte dir, du sollst den Fensterrahmen streichen, nicht die Scheibe!
6. Versuchst du mich zu überzeugen?
7. Ich sah einige wundervolle Gemälde im Museum.

8. Wer warf den Stein nach ihm?
9. Sie haben kein Recht, das zu tun, Jesse.
10. Wenn du das Gesetz brichst, bist du ein Verbrecher.
11. Was war deine Rolle in dem Stück?
12. Steht diese wunderschöne Vase zum Verkauf?
13. Die Stühle sind höher als der Tisch!
14. „Wo sind deine Eltern?" – „Sie sind im Theater."

Exercise 63: Wie lauten folgende Sätze auf Englisch? Unterstreiche alle Homophone, die du entdecken kannst:

1. Er war zu schwach, um aufzustehen.
2. Die Quelle des Flusses ist versiegt.
3. Er musste kein Fahrgeld bezahlen, weil er den Fahrer kannte.
4. Warum sagen Sie mir nicht, wessen Auto das ist?
5. „Diese Arznei wird Ihre Schmerzen lindern", sagte Doktor Taylor.
6. Du bist zu jung zum Heiraten.
7. Ein Stück von dem Puzzle *(jigsaw puzzle)* fehlt!
8. Der Name meines Sohnes ist Frederic.
9. Sein wundes Knie bereitete Herrn Blair viele Schwierigkeiten.
10. Der Mörder kam durch das Küchenfenster herein.
11. Schreibe einen Aufsatz über eines der folgenden Themen *(topic)*:
12. „Warum hältst du nicht an?" – „Ich kann die Bremse nicht finden!"
13. Er kaufte drei Brötchen für seine Enten.
14. Weißt du, wie man ein Segel setzt *(hoist)*?
15. Ich mietete ein Fahrrad, um zum See zu kommen.
16. Warum trägst du deinen Ehering nicht?

Exercise 64: Übersetze die Sätze ins Englische und markiere alle Homophone:

1. Wie bitte? Ich habe nicht gehört, was du sagtest.
2. „Warum erzählen Sie mir nicht die ganze Geschichte?", fragte Holmes.
3. Er wusste sogar meinen Namen!
4. Das ist der Mann, der versucht hat, mir die Brieftasche zu stehlen!
5. Sie fanden eine Leiche unten im Keller.
6. In diesem Theaterstück verlassen Mutter und Tochter den Vater.
7. Der vierte Mann im Zimmer war Doktor Taylor.
8. In der Ferse deiner linken Socke ist ein Loch.
9. Wir begegnen uns jeden Tag an der Bushaltestelle.
10. Meine Mutter hat den ersten Preis bei einem Schönheitswettbewerb gewonnen.
11. Welche Farbe hat dein Haar?
12. Zwei Stunden später traf der Doktor ein.

Exercise 65: Wie lauten die Sätze im Englischen und welche Homophone sind darin enthalten?

1. Warum hast du sie nicht gewarnt?
2. In seiner Angelschnur war ein Knoten.
3. Im Kühlschrank sind keine Eier.
4. Tracy aß zum Frühstück ein paar Weintrauben.
5. „Er ist ein Feigling!" – „Nein, ist er nicht!"
6. „Herr Holmes weiß alles", erklärte Watson dem besorgten Ehemann.
7. Im Eimer ist kein Wasser! Wer hat es verschüttet?
8. Setze das Verb in Klammern in die Vergangenheit.
9. Es ist Viertel nach fünf.
10. Die Sonne ist ein Stern, kein Planet.
11. Es war nicht genug Zeit, die Pistole zu verstecken.
12. Wie viel Gewicht hat sie im Krankenhaus verloren?
13. Auf meinem Weg nach Hause fand ich eine Brieftasche.

14. Er glaubt, dass es Zeitverschwendung ist, in die Schule zu gehen.
15. Er versuchte, den Ast mit einer Säge vom Baum abzuschneiden.
16. Ich werde zu dem Fest gehen, ob es dir gefällt oder nicht.

Exercise 66: Wieder sollst du die Sätze ins Englische übertragen und dann die gefundenen Homophone unterstreichen:

1. Der Hund rannte dem Hasen nach.
2. Der Buchhändler (= -verkäufer) hat mir diesen Roman empfohlen.
3. Er gibt nur eine Antwort, Watson.
4. Mars war der römische Gott des Krieges.
5. Der Koch zeigte mir, wie man das Fleisch richtig schneidet.
6. Die Wunde will *(will)* nicht heilen, Doktor Taylor.
7. Ich wiege genauso viel wie unser Hund.
8. Wir sprachen über das Wetter, die Zukunft und so weiter und so fort.
9. Er schälte die Birne und viertelte sie.
10. Möchtest du etwas Käse zum Nachtisch?
11. Während sie Rotwild jagten, wurden sie von einem Grislibären angegriffen.
12. Wie viele Menschen verloren ihr Leben?
13. Warte auf mich, Roger!
14. Scarlett hatte eine sehr schmale Taille.
15. „Ihr rechtes Bein ist gebrochen, fürchte ich", sagte Doktor Taylor.

8.4 Synonyme

> *Exercise 67:* In dieser Übung sollst du zwei englische Synonyme für jedes der folgenden deutschen Verben finden: *erziehen, lassen, lernen, fahren, machen*. Entscheide dann bei jedem Satzpaar, welches der beiden Synonyme in a.) bzw. b.) eingesetzt werden muss:

1a. I asked John to ... me to the airport.
1b. ... on the Orient Express was his greatest pleasure.
2a. Our neighbour's children have been ... well.
2b. "It's impossible to ... those rebellious children," the teacher complained.
3a. Jennifer ... how to read at the age of four.
3b. In Africa he ... the behaviour of elephants.
4a. I can ... several things at the same time.
4b. Whenever I visit Grandmother, she ... breakfast for me.
5a. After the war he ... the country.
5b. Don't ... Roger play with the dog while I'm away.

> *Exercise 68:* Übersetze folgende Sätze mit Hilfe der eben gefundenen Synonyme ins Englische:

1. Störe deine Schwester nicht! Sie lernt in ihrem Zimmer.
2. Wir fuhren in einem Auto, das keine Klimaanlage *(air-conditioning)* hatte.
3. „Lassen Sie mich Ihr Bein sehen", sagte Doktor Taylor.
4. Bevor ich nach Spanien ging, musste ich Spanisch lernen.
5. Weißt du, wie man Brot macht?
6. Mary wurde von ihrer Großmutter erzogen.
7. Mein Vater fährt ein altes Auto.
8. Lass die Tür offen, es ist zu heiß hier drinnen.
9. Das ist etwas, was ich nie machen würde.
10. Meine Kinder wurden an einer berühmten Schule erzogen.

Exercise 69: Finde je zwei Synonyme für die Verben *leihen, sehen, verdienen, brauchen* und *tragen*. Entscheide bei jedem Satzpaar, welches der beiden in a.) und welches in b.) eingesetzt werden muss:

1a. Does anybody ... the typewriter today?
1b. Why don't you ... a knife and cut the apple into halves?
2a. Every week Miss Marple ... a book or two from her friend.
2b. Of course I have a baseball bat, but I ... it to Roger.
3a. My parents ... television every evening.
3b. When she ... the broken vase she knew what had happened.
4a. Your composition is very good, Sandra. It ... to be read out to the class.
4b. Roger tried to ... some money by walking our neighbour's dog.
5a. My sister ... the basket to the car.
5b. Today our teacher ... his T-shirt the wrong way round.

Exercise 70: Nun übertrage ins Englische und verwende dabei die eben eingesetzten Synonyme:

1. Niemand sah ihn weglaufen.
2. Mein Bruder träumt davon, eines Tages mehr zu verdienen, als er ausgeben kann.
3. Sie lieh mir den besten Regenschirm, den sie hatte.
4. Ich habe diese Zahnbürste nur einmal gebraucht (= benützt).
5. Er verdient die Beförderung, aber einige seiner Kollegen finden (= denken) das nicht.
6. Was brauchst du sonst noch, Roger?
7. Er hatte seinen Regenschirm vergessen, also lieh er sich meinen.
8. Holmes wusste, dass ihm jemand zusah.
9. Der Portier trug unser Gepäck zum Aufzug.

Exercise 71: Diesmal geht es um die Verben *hören, bringen, gehen, erinnern, aufstehen.* Finde je zwei englische Synonyme und trage sie im richtigen Satz (a oder b) ein:

1a. Grandfather ... up from his chair and walked out of the room.
1b. Some of the children at the back of the cinema ... up to see better.
2a. My car broke down so I had to ... home.
2b. Shall we ... shopping this afternoon?
3a. I've ... that Mr and Mrs Richardson are getting divorced!
3b. Nobody ... to what the teacher was saying.
4a. I must ... to walk the dog before I go to school.
4b. I always have to ... Andrew to walk the dog before he goes to school.
5a. Tracy ... her husband to our ladies' party!
5b. ... that knife to Scotland Yard, Watson.

Exercise 72: Wie lauten diese Sätze im Englischen? Verwende dabei die eben gefundenen Synonyme:

1. Bringen Sie mir meine Lupe *(magnifying glass)*, Watson!
2. Um wie viel Uhr stehen die Kinder auf?
3. Dieses Bild erinnert mich an meine Mutter.
4. Roger stand auf, als der Doktor hereinkam.
5. Hört er jemals Radio?
6. Fährst du mit dem Bus oder gehst du?
7. Herr Roberts beschloss seine Frau zum Bahnhof zu bringen.
8. Meine Eltern gehen jeden Sonntag in die Kirche.
9. „Wie viele Schüsse haben Sie an dem Abend gehört?", fragte Holmes.
10. Sie erinnert sich daran, ihm den Autoschlüssel gegeben zu haben.

Exercise 73: Finde für die Verben *besuchen, kochen, aufhören, schauen* und *sagen* je zwei englische Synonyme. Setze sie im richtigen Satzpaar in die entsprechende Lücke ein:

1a. Did Mrs Sutherland ... anything to you about that accident?
1b. Did he ... you the truth?
2a. Every Sunday Doctor Taylor ... to the old lady.
2b. After the sightseeing tour they ... the Natural History Museum.
3a. I can't ... you without my glasses.
3b. Watson was ... in the wrong direction.
4a. First of all you have to ... some water for the spaghetti.
4b. While the potatoes were ..., Mrs Gillingham prepared the fish.
5a. The president ... his speech with a quotation from Shakespeare.
5b. When it ... raining it was too late for our picnic in the country.

Exercise 74: Nun verwende diese Wörter, um folgende Sätze ins Englische zu übersetzen:

1. Warum sagst du nicht, was du denkst?
2. Jeden Abend kocht Frau Taylor für ihre Familie das Abendessen.
3. Judy besucht ihren Onkel in London.
4. Hast du den Film zuvor schon gesehen?
5. Der Film hört mit einer Überraschung auf.
6. Holmes sah aus dem Fenster.
7. Vor drei Wochen habe ich endlich mit dem Rauchen aufgehört.
8. Sag mir, warum du lachst.
9. In unserem Land müssen alle Kinder über fünf die Schule besuchen.
10. Jeden Morgen kocht meine Mutter mir ein Ei.

Exercise 75: Ergänze die Sätze mit je zwei englischen Synonymen für die Substantive *Arbeit, Mann, Himmel, Land* und *Straße*:

1a. What a lovely day! There's not a cloud in the ...!
1b. Grandfather told me that ... is the place where the angels live.
2a. When the company went bankrupt many people lost their ...
2b. She didn't go to the cinema that night because she had a lot of ... to do.
3a. After the flood the ... to London was impassable.
3b. At night the ... in our neighbourhood are empty and quiet.
4a. She fell in love with a handsome ...
4b. Some of the women brought their ... to the party.
5a. How did you get there, by ... or by sea?
5b. When his visa expired, he had to leave the ...

Exercise 76: Verwende beim Übersetzen dieser Sätze die gerade benutzten Synonyme:

1. Hat Frau Grant in Birmingham eine Arbeit als Lehrerin gefunden?
2. Die Straße zum Dorf führt durch einen Wald.
3. Onkel John besitzt ein Stück Land am Meer.
4. Mittags klarte der Himmel wieder auf *(clear up)*.
5. Das Geheimnis meines Erfolgs ist harte Arbeit.
6. Wer ist der Mann mit der langen Nase?
7. Die Brownings wohnen in einer Nebenstraße hinter dem Bahnhof.
8. Auf der Hochzeitsreise war das junge Paar im siebten Himmel.
9. In vielen Ländern ist die Einwanderung gesetzlich beschränkt.
10. Der mit der langen Nase ist mein Mann.

Exercise 77: Finde für die deutschen Substantive *Boden, Spiel, Schatten, Frau* und *Marmelade* je zwei englische Begriffe. Trage sie bei den entsprechenden Satzpaaren an der richtigen Stelle ein:

1a. You'll never get a good tan if you stay in the ...
1b. In the late afternoon a tree casts a long ...
2a. You can use any kind of ... for this cake.
2b. Your grapefruit ... is really sour!
3a. Watson, this suitcase has got a double ...!
3b. Suddenly the ... began to rock under her feet – an earthquake!
4a. Roger introduced the ... to his friends.
4b. Paul's ... wore a red dress at the party.
5a. The Olympic ... were broadcast on television all over the world.
5b. The title of his latest novel is a ... on words.

Exercise 78: Übersetze folgende Sätze mit Hilfe der eben verwendeten Synonyme:

1. Er liebt die Frau eines anderen Mannes.
2. Man braucht zehn Orangen für zwei Gläser *(jar)* Marmelade?
3. Der Boden deines Obstkuchens war ein bisschen trocken.
4. Hören Sie auf, mir zu folgen, Watson! Sie sind doch nicht mein Schatten!
5. Unser Torwart wurde wegen Foulspiels bestraft *(penalize)*.
6. Alice saß auf dem Boden und spielte mit ihrer Puppe.
7. Diese Marmelade ist aus Äpfeln gemacht.
8. Die Kinder spielten ein Ballspiel.
9. Stell das Eis in den Schatten, es schmilzt!
10. Wer ist die Frau, die neben ihm sitzt?

Exercise 79: Finde je zwei englische Synonyme für folgende Substantive: *Preis, Farbe, Gesellschaft, Leben, Reise.* Füge sie in die entsprechenden Sätze ein:

1a. The chameleon can change ... according to its surroundings.
1b. The artist didn't finish the portrait because he had run out of ...
2a. Grandfather spent most of his ... in Africa.
2b. The standard of ... in this country is lower than before the revolution.
3a. The ... of meat is still going up.
3b. The professor was awarded a ... for his recent discovery.
4a. On our ... from Venice to Milan we met many wonderful people.
4b. ... in Africa used to be more dangerous and less comfortable.
5a. I love going out with Thomas and Andrew; I enjoy their ...
5b. Some ... treat children as second-class citizens.

Exercise 80: Wie lauten nachfolgende Sätze im Englischen? Verwende wieder die Synonyme aus Übung 79:

1. Ich ziehe seine Gesellschaft dem Alleinsein vor.
2. Letztes Jahr machten sie eine Reise um die Welt.
3. Die Farbe an der Wand war noch feucht, als Holmes eintraf.
4. Sein Film erhielt einen Preis bei diesem Festival.
5. Nach fünf Jahren wurde er des Lebens im Hotel überdrüssig *(tire).*
6. Mein Großvater schrieb ein Buch über seine Reisen.
7. Eine junge Frau verlor ihr Leben bei dem Unfall.
8. Terrorismus ist eine Bedrohung *(threat)* für die Gesellschaft.
9. Meine Lieblingsfarbe ist Blau.
10. Roger verkaufte sein Auto zu einem guten Preis.

Exercise 81: Grund (für), Paar, Fleisch, während, wie – setze Synonyme für diese Begriffe in die passenden Lücken ein:

1a. It wasn't a ghost who dealt you that blow, Watson, it was a man of ... and blood!
1b. Doctor Taylor told me to eat less ... and more vegetables.
2a. After a ... of miles the two girls grew tired and stopped for a rest.
2b. You ruined my last ... of tights!
3a. "What was the ... his death?" Holmes asked the doctor.
3b. The policeman didn't give any ... arresting them.
4a. A woman fainted ... the magician's performance.
4b. ... he was brushing his teeth the phone rang.
5a. Why didn't he take the car ... I told him?
5b. He cried ... a baby when his beautiful new car broke down.

Exercise 82: Nun verwende die gefundenen Synonyme, um folgende Sätze ins Englische zu übertragen:

1. Dieser Park ist während des Winters geschlossen.
2. Der Grund für dieses Feuer ist vermutlich Brandstiftung *(arson)*.
3. Was für eine Sorte Fleisch ist in dieser Suppe?
4. Lassen Sie alles in diesem Zimmer, wie es ist, Watson.
5. Unsere neuen Nachbarn sind ein junges Paar aus Minnesota.
6. Geh nicht ans Telefon, während ich weg bin.
7. Das Fleisch der gelben Frucht schmeckte süß.
8. Mein jüngerer Bruder sieht ein bisschen wie Huckleberry Finn aus.
9. Aus welchem Grund hat er das gesagt?
10. Meine Mutter kaufte drei Paar Schuhe im Schlussverkauf bei Harrods.

Exercise 83: Jetzt geht es um folgende Adjektive und Adverbien: *falsch, fremd, fertig, klein, schwer.* Finde die englischen Synonympaare und setze sie an der richtigen Stelle ein:

1a. When will she be ... with her work?
1b. The tailor called to say that your wedding dress is ...
2a. "The test was too ... for your son," the teacher said to Mrs Taylor.
2b. Tracy didn't go to school that day because she had a ... cold.
3a. ... friends are not to be trusted.
3b. You're driving on the ... side of the road, Roger! We're in England now!
4a. At the beginning of the international conference ... guests were welcomed in English.
4b. A ... man in a red coat asked me for a light.
5a. He broke his ... finger in the last volleyball match.
5b. There's a ... difference between marmalade and jam.

Exercise 84: Wie lauten die folgenden Sätze im Englischen? Verwende die Synonyme aus Übung 78:

1. Dieser Kleiderschrank ist zu klein für die Kleider meiner Frau.
2. Niemand erkannte Holmes, weil er einen falschen Bart trug.
3. In einer fremden Stadt fühle ich mich immer unwohl.
4. Frau Taylor rief die Kinder, sobald das Abendessen fertig war.
5. Es war schwer für mich, den Ausländer zu verstehen.
6. „Ihr Koffer ist zu schwer, mein Herr", sagte der Mann am Gepäckschalter.
7. Tracy ist so ein süßes kleines Kind.
8. Es ist wichtig, fremde Sprachen in jungen Jahren *(early age)* zu lernen.
9. Unser neues Haus ist beinahe fertig.
10. Sie war so aufgelöst *(upset)*, dass sie die falsche Nummer wählte *(dial)*.

9. Sonstige Fehlerquellen

Exercise 85: Wie lauten folgende Sätze im Englischen? Entscheide, ob das deutsche „wie" mit *how, what* oder *what's ... like* wiedergegeben werden muss:

1. Wie geht es Ihrem Mann, Frau Taylor?
2. Wie spät ist es?
3. Wie wär's mit einem Kaffee?
4. Wie war deine Fahrt nach Italien?
5. Wie ist Tracys Bruder?
6. Wie ist der neue Lehrer?
7. Wie soll das Wetter am Wochenende sein?
8. Wie hast du auf der neuen Matratze geschlafen?
9. Wie wär's, wenn wir in den Zoo gingen?
10. Wie gut ist dein Deutsch?
11. Wie buchstabiert man das Wort „Kuckuck"?
12. Wie war das Konzert gestern Abend?

Exercise 86: Vervollständige die Sätze mit *how, what* oder *what's:*

1. ... the opposite of "weakness"?
2. ... is your wife's Christian name, please?
3. ... many people work here?
4. ... time does the British Airways plane land?
5. ... time is the film on television?
6. ... can he drive when his leg is broken?
7. ... is the German word for "parrot"?
8. ... does it say on the back of the book?
9. ... do you know her name?
10. ... do you usually do after school?
11. ... your opinion of the new teacher?
12. ... do you do, Doctor Taylor?
13. ... are you doing tomorrow?

Exercise 87: Hier geht es um die richtige Übersetzung des Verbs „einladen". Entscheide dich jeweils für eine der folgenden Möglichkeiten: *ask, buy, invite, stand, treat.* In manchen Fällen sind auch zwei Lösungen möglich.

1. I haven't been ... to Tracy's birthday party.
2. Let's go to the pub, I'll ... you a drink.
3. Mr Taylor ... me to a glass of wine.
4. She's ... the Taylors to dinner next Sunday.
5. After the lesson our teacher ... us all to an ice-cream.
6. Shall we ... her new boyfriend to dinner?
7. I'll ... you a drink after the show.
8. The gentleman in the grey suit ... her a cocktail.
9. Grandfather asked the postman in and ... him tea and muffins.
10. Come on, I'll ... you a cup of coffee!
11. They ... us to spend the weekend with them and we accepted.

Exercise 88: Achte beim Übersetzen der vollständigen Sätze darauf, das deutsche „bitte" im Englischen jeweils der Situation entsprechend wiederzugeben:

1. Wer ist bitte am Apparat?
2. Wie bitte? Ich habe nicht gehört, was Sie sagten.
3. „Möchten Sie Tee?" – „Ja, bitte."
4. Zwei Tassen Kaffee, bitte.
5. „Es ist spät." – „Wie bitte?" – „Ich sagte, es ist spät."
6. „Danke, dass du den Hund gefüttert hast." – „Bitte (= gern geschehen)."
7. Nehmen Sie bitte Platz.
8. „Eine Schachtel Zigaretten, bitte." – „Hier, bitte."
9. Darf ich bitte die Lage erklären?
10. „Nehmen Sie noch eine Tasse Kaffee?" – „Ja, bitte."
11. Leg das Papier bitte auf den Tisch.
12. Wie bitte? Was hast du gesagt?
13. „Er ist Rechtsanwalt." – „Wie bitte? Was ist sein Beruf?"

14. „Hier ist der Regenschirm, den Sie vergessen haben." – „Oh, vielen Dank." – „Bitte (= keine Ursache)."
15. „Danke für all Ihre Hilfe." – „Bitte (= nicht der Rede wert)."
16. Können Sie mir bitte den Weg zum Bahnhof zeigen?
17. Kann ich bitte mit dem Geschäftsführer sprechen?
18. „Danke, dass du mich zu der Party gefahren hast." – „Bitte (= es war mir ein Vergnügen)."

Exercise 89: Setze in die Lücken die passende englische Form der Entschuldigung ein:

1. ... I'm late.
2. "Hey, that's my coffee you're drinking!" – "Oh, really? ...!"
3. ..., is this seat taken?
4. "Now you've spilt the beans, Roger!" – "Oh, ...!"
5. ..., did I wake the baby?
6. ..., but I don't think that this is the right way to Birmingham.
7. ..., sir. I've mistaken you for someone else.
8. ... my asking, but aren't you Laura's father?
9. ...! Could you hand me that black coat, please?
10. ... me saying so, but this time your husband is completely wrong.

B. VERMISCHTE TESTS

1. Multiple Choice

Test 1: Wähle die Präposition bzw. den Artikel aus, der in die Lücke gehört:

1. You're not very good ... solving mysteries?
   A. at B. with C. in D. on

2. Did she go there ... bicycle?
   A. on B. with the C. by D. by the

3. This customer is very interested ... archeology.
   A. about B. in C. on D. for

4. My parents used to watch ... television every Friday night.
   A. on B. – C. the

5. It's typical ... Roger to forget his umbrella.
   A. for B. with C. about D. of

6. What did they usually watch ... television?
   A. in B. on the C. on D. in the

7. The actress was very angry ... her poor performance.
   A. with B. at C. about D. of

8. Why don't we go ... the theatre tonight?
   A. to B. at C. into

9. What's wrong ... you, Watson, why are you shivering?
   A. about B. with C. for

10. What play did you see ... the theatre?
    A. in B. at C. on

11. The man over there reminds me ... your brother.
    A. of B. about C. to D. on

12. My children are ... school from 8 a.m. to 1 p.m.
    A. in the B. at C. at the

13. Can you give me a good example ... Romantic poetry?
    A. of B. for C. in D. from

14. How do they get ... school every morning?
    A. to the B. to C. in D. in the

15. Holmes was looking ... a place to hide the letter.
    A. at B. after C. for D. on

16. She didn't recognize herself ... the picture.
    A. in B. on C. at

17. Don't you think you're married ... the wrong man, Jessica?
    A. to B. with C. by

18. I met Mr and Mrs Taylor ... the party.
    A. on B. at C. during D. by

19. I heard the concert ... radio.
    A. in B. on C. on the D. in the

20. The suspect's explanation didn't agree ... Holmes' theory.
    A. with B. about C. on D. to

21. They spent a wonderful day ... the country.
    A. in B. on C. at

22. The time of departure depends ... the weather.
    A. of B. from C. on D. at

23. The old lady insisted ... giving me ten pounds.
    A. – B. to C. on D. upon

Test 2: Setze die richtige Adjektiv- bzw. Substantivform in die Lücke ein:

1. Doctor Taylor's wife is ...
   A. a French B. French C. a Frenchwoman

2. In Atlanta I met three ... from Berlin.
   A. Germans B. Germen C. German

3. The two ... were reunified in 1989.
   A. Germanys B. Germanies C. Germany

4. ... I know are fond of dancing.
   A. The Irish B. Irishmen C. The Irishmen

5. How many ... were at the meeting?
   A. Chinesemen B. Chinese C. Chineses

6. I've ordered us two ...
   A. gins-and-tonics B. gin-and-tonics C. gins and tonic

7. They'll give you ... at the tourist office.
   A. many informations B. plenty of information
   C. much information

8. He put on his ... and went to bed.
   A. pair of pyjamas B. pyjama C. pyjamas

9. After two ... he began to feel a little dizzy.
   A. wines B. glasses of wine C. glass wine

10. How many ... have you got?
    A. trousers B. pairs of trousers C. pairs of trouser

11. John and Derek knew the answer, so they raised ...
    A. the hand B. the hands C. their hands D. their hand

12. Last night our cat caught two ... in the attic.
    A. myce B. mouses C. maice D. mice

Test 3: Trage die erforderliche Adjektiv- bzw. Adverbform in den vorgegebenen Satz ein:

1. It's ... to find our house if you have a map.
   A. more easy B. more easily C. easier D. easyer

2. These exercises are ... easy.
   A. fair B. fairly C. fare D. farely

3. Jennifer was disappointed that she did so ... in the exam.
   A. bad B. worse C. badly

4. Could you speak a bit ...?
   A. more slowly B. slower C. slowlier

5. Doctor Taylor advised me to drink ...
   A. lesser B. lessly C. less D. fewer

6. My mother speaks ... German.
   A. perfect B. perfectly C. most perfect D. most perfectly

7. The plague is a ... contagious *(ansteckend)* disease.
   A. high B. in a high way C. highly

8. Doctor Taylor advised him to go to bed ...
   A. more early B. more earlier C. earlier D. more earlily

9. Are you ... happy with your new car?
   A. truly B. truely C. true

10. Roger and Mary were the ... two students to arrive at the station.
    A. latter B. latest C. last D. most late

11. He slammed the door ...
    A. angry B. angrily C. angryly D. in an angry way

12. Friday was the ... day of the year.
    A. most rainy B. rainiest C. rainyest

13. He was walking too ... for me.
    A. quicker B. quicky C. quickly D. quick

14. That was the ... film I've ever seen!
    A. worse B. worsest C. worst

15. Your illness is ... than I thought.
    A. seriouser B. more seriously C. more serious

16. Holmes was ... convinced of her innocence.
    A. fuly B. in a full way C. fully D. full

17. Why did he ask her ... questions?
    A. so stupid B. such stupid C. so stupidly

18. Her father treated her badly, but her mother treated her even ...
    A. worse B. badder C. more badly D. worser

19. At least he said it ...
    A. friendly B. in a friendly way C. friendlily

20. I tried to explain it as ... as I could.
    A. simply B. simple C. in a simple way

21. When he returned he looked ... than before.
    A. more sadly B. sadder C. sadlier D. more sad

22. The meat was only ... cooked.
    A. halfly B. half C. halvely

23. Do you know a ... child than Emily?
    A. lovelier B. lovelyer C. more lovely

24. Holmes was ... unsure of his theory.
    A. wholly B. whole C. wholely D. wholy

25. You look much ... in the blue dress, Carol.
    A. more pretty B. prettier C. more prettily

Test 4: Setze die richtige Verbform in die Lücke ein:

1. Have you ever ... a Rolls-Royce?
   A. droven B. drived C. driven

2. Last night I ... "Romeo and Juliet".
   A. have seen B. saw C. seen D. sawed

3. She was ... in bed when Doctor Taylor arrived.
   A. lying B. lieing C. laying D. laing

4. Doctor Taylor ... out one hour ago.
   A. went B. has went C. has gone

5. I ... this book when I was at school.
   A. read B. readed C. have read

6. He ... his hands on the table.
   A. lay B. laid C. lied D. layed

7. I ... in three months.
   A. haven't smoked B. haven't smoken C. didn't smoke

8. That girl has just ... five pieces of cake!
   A. eated B. aten C. ate D. eaten

9. Inflation has ... by three percent.
   A. raised B. rised C. risen D. rosen

10. They ... to Tokyo last August.
    A. flied B. flyed C. flew D. flow

11. Holmes ... the letter under the carpet.
    A. hit B. hid C. hided D. hidded

12. How many marbles have you ... so far?
    A. selt B. sold C. selled D. solt

13. I've ... to you about my past, Mr Watson.
    A. laid B. lyed C. lied D. lain

14. Holmes ... his head and pointed at me. "This gentleman is Mr Watson!" he said.
    A. shaked B. shook C. has shaken

15. Have they ... a new president?
    A. choosen B. chosed C. choosed D. chosen

16. Aunt Judy sounded rather ... on the telephone.
    A. hurt B. hurten C. hurted

17. Grandmother wore a hand-... apron *(Schürze)*.
    A. sown B. sewn C. sawn D. sewed E. sowed

18. She ... go to the bank to get some money.
    A. musted B. had to C. needed

19. The "Titanic" ... in 1912 after colliding with an iceberg.
    A. sang B. sunk C. sank D. sinked

20. My grandfather was ... in Berlin in 1899.
    A. born B. bored C. borne

21. He ... in Italy in 1942.
    A. dyed B. died C. dyied

22. She has ... writing a new novel.
    A. begun B. begon C. began

23. The water in our swimming-pool was ...
    A. freezed B. frost C. frozen D. frosted

24. After a short rest she ... much better.
    A. feelt B. felled C. feeled D. fell E. felt

25. Someone has ... a branch off the maple tree!
    A. sawn B. sown C. sowed D. sewn

Test 5: Nun geht es um vermischte Wortschatzprobleme. Setze den bzw. die richtigen Begriffe in die Lücke ein:

1. My bicycle had a puncture and so I had to change the ...
   A. heel B. wheel C. heal D. he'll

2. She was in her room the ... time.
   A. whole B. haul C. hole D. howl

3. Your father was ... yesterday.
   A. her B. hear C. here D. heir

4. Roger ... the best business school in New York.
   A. visits B. attends C. goes to

5. You can't go for a walk in this ...
   A. wether B. weather C. whether D. wheather

6. I ... a lot of mistakes on the test.
   A. took B. did C. made

7. Mr Barnes usually ... to work by car.
   A. drives B. rides C. goes

8. I haven't got enough time to ... the work.
   A. end B. stop C. finish D. ready

9. Soccer is a very boring ...
   A. game B. play C. match

10. You'd better ... early tomorrow.
    A. get up B. stand up C. rise

11. I was the ... to realize the danger.
    A. onliest B. only one C. only

12. My sister can sing quite ...
    A. well B. good C. welly D. goodly

13. He's got ... money in the bank.
    A. a lot of B. much C. many

14. Buses to Flagstaff run ... two hours.
    A. each B. every C. any

15. ...? What did you say?
    A. Excuse me B. Sorry C. Please

16. ... suitcase was checked at customs.
    A. Any B. Some C. Every

17. I used to ... a lot of fishing when I was a bachelor.
    A. do B. make C. take

18. Give me the key, please. – ...
    A. You're welcome B. Here you are C. Please

19. "You're standing on my foot!" – "Who, ...?"
    A. I B. me C. myself

20. No, not you! ..., with the black umbrella!
    A. She B. Herself C. Her D. Hers

21. I want you two to apologize to ... other!
    A. every B. each C. any

22. Could you ... me the time, please?
    A. say B. speak C. tell

23. The new teacher ... us all to doughnuts.
    A. spended B. invited C. treated

24. They lived here ... for two years.
    A. happy B. happily C. lucky D. luckily

25. ... of them had an alibi, so both of them were arrested by the police.
    A. either B. neither C. any D. each

26. Did Roger catch ...?
   A. any fishes B. some fish C. any fish D. some fishes

27. Mrs Taylor looked ... our children well.
   A. for B. after C. to

Test 6: Diesmal geht es darum, das einzige Wort zu finden, das nicht in die Lücke passt:

1. Have you read the ... opinion polls?
   A. latest B. current C. actual

2. The ... at the box-office told me that the show had sold out.
   A. woman B. wife C. lady

3. ... student had a pocket calculator.
   A. Every B. Each C. Any

4. Even his secretary ... more money than I do!
   A. becomes B. gets C. earns

5. ... my husband will take me to the station.
   A. Maybe B. Eventually C. Perhaps

6. Tracy is as ... as her brother.
   A. big B. gross C. tall

7. The car was much ... than the motorbike.
   A. faster B. quicker C. rasher

8. Our new baby-sitter is such a ... girl.
   A. sympathetic B. nice C. likeable

9. The ... of this exercise is to increase your English vocabulary.
   A. aim B. zeal C. purpose

10. Jennifer ... me her prettiest dress.
    A. gave B. lent C. borrowed

11. Father was ... the heavy suitcase upstairs.
    A. carrying B. wearing C. lugging

12. The teacher assigned us a very ... exercise.
    A. tricky B. heavy C. difficult

13. Did you enjoy your last ...?
    A. travel B. journey C. tour

14. Why are you ... that woman as she crosses the street?
    A. seeing B. watching C. looking at

15. The shop assistant ... that the woman had bought an umbrella.
    A. reminded B. remembered C. recalled

16. The ... for her suicide is still unclear.
    A. cause B. motive C. reason

17. Can I ... to your mother, please?
    A. speak B. say C. talk

18. How many different ... of butterflies can you name?
    A. sorts B. arts C. kinds

19. When he entered the room a dozen ... faces turned towards him.
    A. foreign B. unfamiliar C. strange

20. The little girl lay on the ... and wept.
    A. bottom B. floor C. ground

21. The truck driver ... me a beer.
    A. bought B. stood C. spent

2. Fehlertexte

Test 7: In jedem der folgenden Sätze verbirgt sich ein falsches bzw. falsch geschriebenes Wort. Finde es und ersetze es durch den richtigen englischen Begriff:

1. He studied Italian in a few months.
2. You're happy to have got a seat at all, Madam.
3. When the pane returned, he took another pill.
4. The onliest thing she hasn't got is a fur coat.
5. They waisted hours looking for a meteor.
6. These flowers don't become enough sun.
7. What did she make with her old car?
8. "Did you eventually see the crime happen?" Holmes inquired.
9. Christopher always wrote love letters while his biology lessons.
10. Mrs Whistler brought her children to school before she went shopping.
11. Our new school looks rather like a fabric.
12. She through his new tie away because she didn't like the colour.
13. Let the wet toys outside!
14. I don't like the paint of your new car.
15. The two sisters went from Pasadena to Anaheim in three hours.
16. May I watch the book, please?
17. She boiled scrambled eggs for her brother.
18. I could have borrowed you my spectacles.
19. My father showed me how to drive a motorbike when I was fourteen years old.
20. She criticized my weigh of living.
21. Could you speak clearer, please?
22. Your right – it's raining!
23. I'm afraid there isn't some pudding left.
24. He left his wive for a night-club singer.
25. My children speak German very good.
26. Roger teached his parrot to fly through a hoop.

Test 8: In den folgenden Sätzen sind jeweils mindestens zwei Begriffe falsch bzw. falsch geschrieben. Welche Wörter sind es und wie müssen sie richtig lauten?

1. Tracy hasn't started working still. She's yet in high school.
2. She was educated on the land; that's why she likes land live.
3. The actress refused too play the roll of the mother in the new play.
4. They boiled there steaks over the fire.
5. During she was wandering weather to buy the boots or not, someone else came and bought them.
6. He ate another peace off cake.
7. My mother's been doing homework all morning and she's not ready yet.
8. In most lands children start school with six.
9. She had to go home because she had no money for her bus fair.
10. The mens risked their life to save the three childs from drowning.
11. Doctor Taylor was so happy if his daughter won the price.
12. My man's hairs are getting grey.
13. I heard his song in the radio last weak.
14. What's the best serie in TV?
15. How was you're fly to Detroit?
16. I'll buy potatos as soon as the prize comes down.
17. The kind was playing with a knive.
18. There were two men sitting in the boot; one of them stood up and winked at me.
19. When he came back, he found a complete foreigner standing in the gang.
20. She was to week to carry the suitcase upstairs.
21. "Did you tramp to Amsterdam?" – "No, I drove there by train."
22. The shop assistant refused to exchange the short because I had bought it during the sail.
23. My children don't eat many fruits.
24. This trouser is to big for you.
25. They're showing the rugby play life in TV!
26. The police hasn't found the murder yet.

27. The cattles geted out of the field because the gate wasn't shut.
28. She wanted to have any piece, that's why she didn't answer the phone.

3. Lückentexte

Test 9: In jedem Satz befindet sich eine Lücke. Fülle sie mit Hilfe des deutschen Begriffes in Klammern, der ins Englische zu übertragen ist:

1. The hired car had bad ... (Bremsen)
2. The film started at five ... seven. (nach)
3. Mrs Taylor was ... a white skirt. (tragen)
4. It's a ... task, Watson. (schwer)
5. Harrods is a very famous ... (Warenhaus)
6. We'll ... the Blairs on Friday. (treffen)
7. The ... was black with clouds. (Himmel)
8. She had to buy more ... for the kitchen. (Farbe)
9. Roger is ... than his brother. (kleiner)
10. Liverpool is an interesting ... (Stadt)
11. Ironing is a ... I don't like. (Arbeit)
12. Espresso is a ... of coffee. (Art)
13. We went ... school together. (zur)
14. Can you ... me an umbrella, please? (leihen)
15. I think they should show more basketball ... television. (im)
16. I'll ask Roger if I can ... his baseball bat. (sich leihen)
17. Our school is a ..., ugly building. (groß)
18. He showed me a photo ... his daughter. (von)
19. Yesterday the temperature in the ... was 33 degrees! (Schatten)
20. This ... leads from San Francisco to Los Angeles. (Straße)
21. Mr Blair's ... is a famous actress. (Frau)
22. My parents fly to Paris ... year. (jedes)
23. My wife was ... the housework. (machen)

24. My sister is very shy in ... (Gesellschaft)
25. "Don't worry, it's only a ...-wound," Doctor Taylor said. (Fleisch-)
26. Tracy is a diligent girl but her brother is rather ... (faul)
27. She cooked the ... in boiling water. (Kohl)
28. The two policemen were running ... our house. (vorbei an)
29. They ... the President's speech on CNN. (senden)
30. Professor Munroe is a ... scientist. (genial)
31. The ... were howling all night. (Wölfe)
32. He turned down the ... street. (falsch)
33. She put sugar into the ... instead of salt. (Soße)
34. Holmes asked her if she had a ... heart. (schwach)

Test 10: Die folgenden Sätze haben mehrere Lücken. Um sie füllen zu können, musst du die Begriffe in Klammern ins Englische übersetzen:

1. The old lady tried to ... the suitcase but it was ... (tragen, zu schwer)
2. The ... will drown if you ... them alone in the ..., Pamela! (Babys, lassen, Bad)
3. Hurry up! Your ... will be furious ... you're late. (Chef, wenn)
4. I promise to walk the dog ... the rain ... (wenn, aufhören)
5. She admitted that she was never good ... biology ... school. (in, in der)
6. My ...'s very good ... English. (Sohn, in)
7. Mrs Taylor's ... ... more money than she does. (Mann, verdienen)
8. The taxi driver gave us ... useful ... (viele, Informationen)
9. ... she knew the answer, she'd win a beautiful ... (wenn, Oldtimer)
10. Our teacher wants us to ... more ... (machen, Hausaufgaben)
11. That's the house ... my grandmother was ... (wo, geboren)
12. Our ... was examined at .... (Gepäck, Zoll)

13. I've been ... Paris for two weeks but so far I haven't had time to ... the Louvre. (in, besuchen)
14. Don't you think she's ... old to ... that ... of ...? (zu, tragen, Art, Hut)
15. The plane took off and the people on the ... ... goodbye. (Boden, winken)
16. Obviously, the burglar had cut a ... in the ... door. (Loch, Stahl-)
17. I'm tired of climbing up ... ... (diese, Treppe)
18. She tied a ... in her handkerchief, hoping that it would ... her to feed the cat. (Knoten, erinnern)
19. "Did you notice that the shoes he ... weren't a ...?" Holmes asked his assistant. (tragen, Paar)
20. It was very ... of you ... help me up the stairs. (gütig, zu)
21. "Which pen do you want?" – "The ..." (grünen)

4. *Übersetzungen*

Test 11: Wie lauten die folgenden Sätze im Englischen?

1. Was machst du normalerweise am Wochenende?
2. Findest du nicht, dass dieser Rock etwas zu locker sitzt *(be)*?
3. Als Krieg ausbrach, verließ er das Land sofort.
4. Als sie den Dom gesehen hatten, besuchten sie das Museum.
5. Wie war das Wetter während Ihres Urlaubs?
6. Jedes Jahr besucht sie ein neues Land.
7. Wenn du fertig bist, bringe ich den Kaffee herein.
8. Roger bekommt zu viel Taschengeld.
9. Nachts kamen die Mäuse aus ihren Löchern.
10. Einige der Spieler verbrachten den Tag vor dem großen Spiel auf dem Land.
11. Über welche Hose sprechen wir (eigentlich), die rote oder die blaue?
12. Du brauchst den jungen Hund nicht zu tragen, er kann sehr gut laufen.

13. Letztes Ostern trampte Roger nach Venedig.
14. Meine neue Arbeit ist viel schlimmer, als ich erwartet hatte.
15. Sie hatten keine Streichhölzer, also konnten sie kein Feuer anzünden.
16. Er wurde ins Gefängnis geschickt, weil er sich weigerte, das Bußgeld zu bezahlen.
17. Es war schwer, die Landkarte im Regen zu lesen.
18. Ich bin mit der Zeitung noch nicht fertig.
19. Er hat viel Freizeit, aber ich habe nicht viel (Freizeit).
20. Er verließ den Pub, ohne sein Bier zu bezahlen.
21. Unser Nachbar sagt, es werde dieses Jahr keine Birnen geben.

Test 12: Übersetze nachstehende Sätze ins Deutsche:

1. An ambulance took the pregnant woman to hospital.
2. They found him guilty and sent him to prison.
3. She gave the dog some of her biscuits.
4. I must go to the bank tomorrow.
5. They usually box in the gymnasium.
6. She spends all her money on clothes.
7. Roger isn't capable of earning a living.
8. Yesterday the new teacher gave a lecture.
9. It's lucky the car isn't damaged.
10. Actually, Peter was the one who did it.
11. Your father is a very sensible man.
12. I missed the train and consequently I was late.
13. My new car is as fast as yours.
14. The apple you gave me was rotten.
15. His rude behaviour annoyed my parents.
16. As a child Mary was quite self-conscious.
17. He's a genial man; he always helps me with the gardening.
18. He wrote his name on a blank piece of paper.
19. It was a lovely day and so they went for a walk.
20. The old lady kept all her savings in this box.

Test 13: Übertrage die Sätze ins Englische:

1. Mein Sohn verbringt Stunden damit fernzusehen.
2. Anthony arbeitete hart in der Schule, daher bekam er eine gute Stelle, als er abging *(leave)*.
3. Holmes nahm die Drohung nicht ernst.
4. Der Fotograf hatte seit Jahren keine Bilder mehr gemacht.
5. Wie war das Konzert gestern?
6. Entschuldigen Sie bitte, dass ich zu spät komme.
7. Wie bitte? Das habe ich nicht gehört.
8. Ich lasse dich nicht fernsehen, bevor du dein Abendessen aufgegessen (= beendet) hast.
9. Musst du es selbst bezahlen?
10. Erinnerst du dich noch an deinen ersten Schultag, Jennifer?
11. Er putzte seine Schuhe blank, bevor er ging.
12. Unser Nachbar hat einen großen Hund.
13. Sei nicht so faul! Steh auf und hilf deinem Vater!
14. Es ist nicht sehr taktvoll, über seine Nase zu lachen.
15. Du rauchst ja wieder! Du bist nicht sehr konsequent, oder?
16. Ich habe mir die aktuelle Ausgabe von „Newsweek" gekauft.
17. Ich war glücklich, als ich Großmutter wieder sah.
18. In dieser Bowle ist zu viel Zucker.

Test 14: Wie lauten folgende Sätze auf Deutsch?

1. He warned us not to walk on the ice.
2. "I wish it would rain," said the farmer.
3. Have you enrolled for a course?
4. He was bitten by a snake in the forest.
5. Do you think it's better to educate children at home?
6. When she left school she became a greengrocer.
7. It was very brave of you to go back into the burning house.

8. Tom can't run as fast as I can.
9. Before signing the contract he calculated the cost.
10. What's the name of the company you hired your video recorder from?
11. The two actors hardly spoke at all.
12. I wonder how they knew about his accident.
13. He swam quite near the bank for fear of the current.
14. "Clear up this mess before you go fishing!" his mother called.
15. As soon as he had earned some money he spent it at the races.
16. The accident happened just as I was fastening my seatbelt.
17. He didn't ask her to lunch because he was very busy.
18. It would cost millions to rebuild the dome.
19. Grandfather showed us how to light a fire without matches.
20. What do you prefer, playing in matches or watching them?

Test 15: Übersetze vom Deutschen ins Englische:

1. Er war viel gütiger zu seinem ältesten Sohn als zu den anderen.
2. Die Kinder spielten auf der Straße, als ihre Eltern zurückkehrten.
3. Wir flogen gerade über die Wüste, als ein Sturm losbrach *(break)*.
4. Watson erhielt einen Schlag auf den Kopf und sank zu Boden.
5. Es ist mir unmöglich, zu Hause zu lernen.
6. Einige aus der Gruppe kannten den Weg nicht.
7. Meine Frau war eine Woche lang krank und während dieser Woche hat sie nichts gegessen.
8. Der Lehrer sagte: „Ihr dürft gehen, wenn ihr fertig seid."
9. Denken Sie, dass der Zug pünktlich sein wird?
10. Würdest du dich um meine Goldfische kümmern, während ich weg bin?

11. Als er eintraf, war sie noch immer dabei, das Essen zu kochen.
12. Ich habe 200 Flaschen italienischen Wein in meinem Keller.
13. Du solltest weniger Fleisch essen, wenn du abnehmen (= Gewicht verlieren) willst.
14. Sonntags stand Großvater immer früh auf und ging wandern.
15. Sie konnten es sich nicht leisten, in der Stadt zu leben.
16. Es ist leichter, Chinesisch zu sprechen als es zu schreiben.
17. Sie vergeudete einen ganzen Nachmittag damit, nach der Quittung zu suchen.
18. Sie backte einen Biskuitkuchen für das Gartenfest.
19. Diese Äpfel sehen köstlich aus! Ich nehme acht von den roten.
20. Am Ende fand sie heraus, was mit dem Auto nicht stimmte.

Lösungen

Teil A

Exercise 1:
strawberries, journeys, leaves, guys, ladies, buses, buzzes, kisses, hoofs/hooves, quizzes, issues, menus, halves, flies, teeth, proofs, mice, lice, roofs, canoes, wives, loaves, chiefs, safes

Exercise 2:
1. fish; There is one fish in the pond. 2. dice; You need one dice for this game. 3. scarfs/scarves; She bought one scarf yesterday. 4. tomatoes and cherries; I've eaten one tomato and one cherry. 5. echoes; I can hear one echo. 6. sheep; One sheep has been killed by the wolf. 7. wolves; One wolf has been shot.

Exercise 3:
goose, lorry, zero, body, hero, man, penny, volcano, crisis, radio, axe, holiday, tornado, studio, self, kangaroo, penny, mosquito

Exercise 4:
1. One bag of potatoes weighs ten kilos.
2. This farmer has got five chickens and eight head of cattle: three calves, three cows and two oxen.
3. "Have you got children?" – "Yes, I have two babies. They are twins."
4. Every morning the boys must brush their teeth.
5. Be careful of those knives!
6. Eight people lost their lives in the accident.
7. He's got big feet, and his left foot is even bigger than the right one.
8. The new TV programme lasts one and a half hours.

Exercise 5:
1. I tried to help him, but he doesn't want any advice.
2. Doctor Burns gave me some good advice.
3. I'm sorry, but I can't give you any further information.
4. I need some information.
5. The furniture in Miss Simpson's house is rather extravagant.
6. I bought several pieces of furniture for our living-room.
7. My father's hair is getting grey.
8. Waiter! There's a hair in my soup!
9. Is this good news or bad news?
10. There's only one piece of luggage left.
11. Harold used to watch the news every evening.
12. "Where's your luggage, madam?" the doorman asked.

Exercise 6:
1. I need a new pair of trousers. These trousers are too big for me.
2. I can't find my glasses. Do you know where they are?
3. "How much are these scissors?" – "Ten dollars." – "Ten dollars for one pair of scissors?"
4. I got high marks in all subjects except mathematics and physics.
5. Yesterday my brother fell down the stairs and broke a rib.
6. "Your lungs are as white as snow," the doctor said with a smile.
7. "All of your clothes were stolen?" – "No, just one dress and a pair of shorts."

Exercise 7:
1. Leute; 2. die Völker; 3. beim Zoll; 4. die Sitten und Bräuche; 5. Manieren; 6. Art; 7. Politik; 8. Kunstwerk; 9. hinter dem Wasserwerk; 10. Alter; 11. Ewigkeiten; 12. Schnaps; 13. Teamgeist

Exercise 8:
1. The Japanese; 2. a Spaniard; 3. Spanish; 4. Italians; 5. French; 6. Scottish; 7. German; 8. American; 9. The Swiss; 10. Switzerland; 11. an Englishman; 12. France; 13. Turkey, Turkish

Exercise 9:
1. He's Greek; his wife is Turkish, but she speaks Greek.
2. Two Greeks asked me where the station is.
3. The Irish call their island "Eire".
4. I met three Swiss and a Spaniard in the Himalayas.
5. My daughter is good at German, but she is even better at French.
6. The United States are in North America.
7. Wine is much cheaper in France than in Germany.
8. They spent their holidays in Austria last year.
9. Have you ever been to Australia?
10. Does the word "Zeitgeist" exist in English?
11. I'm sorry but I don't speak Japanese, and I don't speak Chinese, either.
12. He speaks Bavarian, that's why you can't understand him.
13. He told me a joke about an Englishman and a Frenchman.

Exercise 10:
1. "Who is it?" – "It's us! Tom and Mary!"
2. "Have you eaten my cake?" – "Who, me?"
3. There are three hospitals in this city.
4. I asked Mary but she didn't know.
5. I'm glad your mother is feeling better.
6. "How are you, Mr Jekyll?" – "Oh, I'm fine, thank you, Mr Hyde."
7. Put on your shoes before you go.
8. If I were him I wouldn't do it.
9. Look at that dog over there! It's chasing the postman!
10. "Who are those people?" – "They are my friends."
11. I'm sorry I'm late.

Exercise 11:
1. much; 2. any, 3. many; 4. any, some; 5. any; 6. many; 7. Some; 8. some; 9. any; 10. any; 11. many; 12. much, much, a lot of; 13. some, many; 14. any

Exercise 12:
1. Each; 2. either; 3. Every; 4. each; 5. neither; 6. Each; 7. Each/Every one; 8. each; 9. either; 10. neither; 11. Every; 12. either; 13. Each/Every one

Exercise 13:
1. She hates everything yellow.
2. A pessimist is always prepared for the worst.
3. The accused refused to admit his guilt.
4. The wounded and the sick were taken to the nearest hospital.
5. "I'll take the big one!" Jimmy exclaimed, pointing at the huge teddy bear in the corner.
6. "The odd thing is that the dead woman was found in the kitchen," said Watson.
7. Robin Hood took money from the rich and gave it to the poor.
8. The dead were buried in a hurry because a storm was coming.
9. Those present didn't notice the spider.

Exercise 14:
1. He's the most famous actor in this country.
2. It was the most interesting performance of the evening.
3. This is the oldest house in our town.
4. My son is the best student in his class.
5. Tracy is the most beautiful girl I've ever seen.
6. It was the happiest day in his life.
7. You're the worst football player I know.
8. Grandpa told us the funniest story I've ever heard.
9. Wednesday was the hottest day of the year.
10. She wore the prettiest dress she had.
11. She bought the ugliest handbag in the shop.
12. Marrying her was the most stupid thing he's ever done.
13. The girl stole the most expensive watch she could find.

Exercise 15:
1. sadder; 2. harder; 3. elder, older; 4. longer, angrier; 5. worse; 6. busier; 7. less; 8. better; 9. cheaper; 10. sooner, earlier; 11. drier, wetter; 12. more, hungrier

Exercise 16:
1a. Newsweek is a weekly magazine.
1b. This magazine is published weekly.
2a. He's got a friendly smile.
2b. He smiled at me in a friendly way.
3a. The Millers are on their yearly trip to Spain.
3b. The Nobel Prize is awarded yearly.
4a. We had an early lunch.
4b. We had lunch early.
5a. Ann's got a lovely voice.
5b. She sang the song in a lovely way.
6a. Look at that ugly dog!
6b. It bares its teeth in an ugly manner.
7a. I enjoyed my daily visits to Grandma.
7b. I used to visit Grandma daily.
8a. I don't like that silly boy.
8b. Whenever I meet him he looks at me in a silly manner.

Exercise 17:
1. only, late; 2. fair, fairly, pretty; 3. fairly, ill; 4. closely, hardly; 5. lately; 6. only; 7. highly; 8. well, more prettily; 9. well, ill; 10. nearly; 11. near, just; 12. just; 13. most; 14. mostly

Exercise 18:
1. already; 2. still; 3. yet; 4. still; 5. yet; 6. already; 7. still; 8. already; 9. still; 10. already; 11. yet

Exercise 19:
1. Mary is still in bed.
2. Is it midnight already?
3. It hasn't stopped raining yet.
4. It's still raining.
5. We haven't had dinner yet.
6. She was already there when her parents arrived.
7. Paul is still here.
8. Paul hasn't gone yet.

Exercise 20:
1. do; 2. made; 3. do; 4. doing; 5. take; 6. make; 7. do; 8. did; 9. take; 10. made; 11. took; 12. took; 13. did; 14. take; 15. takes; 16. doing; 17. do; 18. make; 19. do; 20. took

Exercise 21:
1. wonder; 2. am surprised; 3. complained; 4. behaving; 5. fell in love; 6. gave in; 7. rely; 8. meet; 9. got dressed/dressed, combed, brushed his teeth; 10. are afraid

Exercise 22:
1. Seeing, getting; 2. kidnapped; 3. doing, dyeing; 4. bathing; 5. flying; 6. stopped, hopping; 7. pitied; 8. digging, zigzagged; 9. travelled; 10. baking, dying; 11. fulfilled; 12. staying; 13. coming; 14. studying; 15. X-rayed

Exercise 23:
1. He came from Frankfort.
2. It took half an hour to get to the airport.
3. He left his wife seven years ago.
4. I met Judy at the station.
5. No, I ate some mousse.
6. I bought a wedding dress at Harrods.
7. The dress cost a fortune.
8. I tried to eat a mouse.
9. The teacher spoke to John's parents.
10. He told them some bad news.
11. Mary put her glasses on the desk.
12. I threw her glasses away because they were broken.
13. I found a dozen marbles that day.
14. No, he listened to the ten o'clock news.

Exercise 24:
1. seen, saw; 2. drunk, drank; 3. bitten, bit; 4. written, wrote; 5. paid, paid; 6. driven, drove; 7. risen, rose; 8. found, found; 9. caught, caught; 10. rung, rang; 11. fed, fed; 12. drawn, drew

Exercise 25:
Dear Kathy,
Lots of things have happened during the past few months. My brother Henry has gone to Rome. My father has found a new job, and my mother has given up smoking. She has sold her old Chrysler and bought a new car. And she has taught me how to drive, isn't that great? By the way, have I told you about our last trip to the countryside? It was a nightmare. Tom fell from a tree and broke his leg, I caught a cold and Mary cut her feet on some pieces of broken glass. A farmer drove us to the nearest hospital where a doctor sewed up Mary's cuts. A nurse put Tom's arm in plaster and felt my pulse. She gave me some antibiotics and I grew tired. So I lay down and took a nap. I slept until the doctor woke me up. I rose in a hurry, looked across the room and saw – our parents! They had come to take us home. We left and flew back to San Francisco immediately. Believe me, country life is dangerous!
Love,
Lucy

Exercise 26:
1. haven't spent; They last spent a weekend together in January.
2. held; They haven't held a meeting for one month.
3. haven't driven; I last drove to Scotland three years ago.
4. brought; You haven't brought me flowers since our wedding day.
5. fed; Tom hasn't fed the cat for two days!
6. hasn't slept; Jerry last slept on a water-bed when he was a bachelor.
7. swam; The children haven't swum in the ocean for four weeks.

8. swept; The cleaning woman hasn't swept the floor since Friday.
9. shot; The poacher hasn't shot a rabbit since May.
10. haven't rung; I last rang him up the day I met you.
11. wore; I haven't worn these glasses since 1966.
12. haven't wound; I last wound this watch on Wednesday.
13. built; I haven't built a sand-castle since I was five years old.
14. sang; She hasn't sung this aria since she was a teenager.
15. hasn't bought; My wife last bought a new dress in spring.
16. drank; I haven't drunk coffee for two weeks.
17. broke down; The car hasn't broken down for two months.

Exercise 27:
1. rode, fell, broke; 2. threw, smelt; 3. rose, began; 4. shut; 5. hid; 6. taught; 7. forgave; 8. broadcast; 9. stood, read; 10. took out, lit; 11. held, shook; 12. felt; 13. wore, thought; 14. spoke; 15. tore out; 16. carried; 17. hurt

Exercise 28:
1. stuck; 2. sat, bent; 3. chosen; 4. didn't know, knew, have you known; 5. fled, sounded; 6. shone; 7. spoilt; 8. struck; 9. braked, broke; 10. swore, seen; 11. wrung; 12. bore; 13. born; 14. loaded; 15. laden; 16. hung; 17. hanged; 18. swung, spun; 19. bought, stolen

Exercise 29:
1. to; 2. of; 3. at; 4. by; 5. of; 6. in; 7. to; 8. to; 9. of; 10. about; 11. by; 12. with; 13. at; 14. by; 15. at

Exercise 30:
1. surprised by; 2. bad at; 3. different from; 4. disappointed with; 5. wrong with; 6. good at; 7. impressed by; 8. is afraid of; 9. interested in; 10. kind to; 11. married to; 12. surprised at; 13. typical of; 14. angry with; 15. angry about

Exercise 31:
1. reminded, of; 2. looking after; 3. agreed to; 4. believe in; 5. thinks about; 6. depends on; 7. dreamed of; 8. insisted on; 9. listen to; 10. looked at; 11. agree with; 12. pay for; 13. reminded, to; 14. shouts at; 15. arrived in; 16. smiled at; 17. suffer from; 18. took part in; 19. looking for; 20. apologized for; 21. congratulated, on

Exercise 32:
1. of; 2. in; 3. with; 4. for; 5. about; 6. after; 7. in; 8. in; 9. for; 10. on; 11. to; 12. for; 13. at; 14. with, from; 15. to; 16. on; 17. at; 18. of; 19. on; 20. at; 21. to

Exercise 33:
1. at; 2. by; 3. at; 4. in; 5. on; 6. at; 7. in; 8. on; 9. on; 10. by; 11. at; 12. at; 13. In; 14. in; 15. at; 16. by; 17. by

Exercise 34:
1. I hope the train will arrive on time.
2. My children are at school all morning.
3. "Romeo and Juliet" is a play by Shakespeare.
4. I saw the game on television last Friday.
5. We spent the weekend in the country.
6. My mother is not at home. She's at the theatre.
7. I met Janet in the city last night.
8. My car is the blue one at the end of the street.
9. Dorothy is going to Islington by bus.
10. Have you read about the accident in the paper?
11. My sister is studying biology at university.
12. I heard the news on the radio.

13. Last night I was at the cinema.
14. My children go to school by bike.
15. We can go to Bristol by train.
16. There were many people at the party.
17. Who is the other girl in the picture?

Exercise 35:
1. When he's read the book I can have it.
2. If you heat ice, it melts.
3. You can take my umbrella if you like.
4. When the weather is hot the beaches are crowded.
5. The teacher will be annoyed if I'm late.
6. When the rain stops I'll go to the zoo.
7. If I had a ruler I would lend it to you.
8. Do you mind if I take your umbrella?
9. I'll ask John when I get home from school.
10. If I were you, I wouldn't apologize for it.

Exercise 36:
1. when; 2. if; 3. If; 4. when; 5. if; 6. If; 7. If; 8. when; 9. When; 10. when; 11. If; 12. When; 13. When; 14. If

Exercise 37:
1. Paul Whistler is a doctor.
2. He is Doctor Paul Whistler.
3. God spoke to Moses.
4. Apollo was the Greek god of music.
5. Is he a minister?
6. He is the Prime Minister.
7. Her Majesty the Queen gave a speech on Friday.
8. Elizabeth II was crowned queen in 1953 at Westminster Abbey.
9. Oh, I love Christmas pudding!
10. What's the name of this street? Is it Baker Street?
11. Your aunt bought a German car last August. Who, Aunt Judy?
12. Is Sir Andrew a member of the Church of England?
13. Penguins live at the South Pole.
14. Starlings fly south for winter.
15. Two members of the Labour Party came to my birthday party.

Exercise 38:
1. Reverend Adams told us to sing the Lord's Prayer.
2. My uncle's car is a Ford.
3. My grandfather lost his life in the Second World War.
4. Mary went to a cinema at Washington Square to see "The Silence of the Lambs".
5. The President of the United States received three Members of Parliament at the White House.
6. The president of our committee lives in a white house.

Exercise 39:
1. hatte Glück; 2. der eigentliche Grund; 3. das darauf folgende Gelächter; 4. schnell; 5. faulig; 6. Bruttoeinkommen; 7. Schüssel; 8. auch; 9. gehemmt; 10. ein freundlicher Empfang; 11. ein leeres Blatt Papier; 12. vernünftig

Exercise 40:
1. Janet was happy with her new car.
2. Miniskirts are always up-to-date.
3. Your son is a very sensitive child.
4. He's very consistent: he eats neither meat nor eggs.

5. I'm almost five years old.
6. We live in a large house.
7. The punch was served in a bowl.
8. Roger was ill so he stayed at home.
9. Martin is more self-confident than his brother.
10. My grandfather was a brilliant scientist.
11. He polished his shoes before he left.
12. Don't be so lazy!

Exercise 41:
1. mollig; 2. schließlich; 3. ein berühmter Künstler; 4. schuldig; 5. mitfühlend; 6. Sei tapfer! 7. haben Sie ein paar Minuten für mich Zeit; 8. blinzelte mir zu; 9. wurden; 10. verbringen; 11. drehte sich um

Exercise 42:
1. Our new neighbours are quite nice, don't you think so?
2. Perhaps Susan and Roger will drop in tonight.
3. That's an excellent idea!
4. I'm sorry, but your ticket is no longer valid.
5. Henry and Martha were well-behaved children.
6. The girl waved when her friends entered the room.
7. The winner donated the money to Greenpeace.
8. This painting is a clumsy forgery.
9. My brother is saving for a new car.
10. Roger is very good at gymnastics.
11. He received a letter from his girlfriend.

Exercise 43:
1. schließen; 2. hat sich eingeschrieben; 3. wanderten im Wald umher; 4. habe ich ausgeschlafen; 5. erteilte ihm die Absolution; 6. ich wünsche; 7. die Kosten; 8. Kuppel; 9. Staffeleien; 10. Wollstoff; 11. Vorsicht; 12. diesen kleinen Hund/dieses Hündchen; 13. Koch

Exercise 44:
1. Stop playing with your dolls!
2. The hedgehog rolled up and fell asleep.
3. He completed the course in less than two months.
4. She wiped away her tears and tried to smile.
5. Many Christians fast to prepare for the Easter festival.
6. Can you ride a donkey?
7. Many men in our neighbourhood work in the factory.
8. He didn't pay the deposit so I let the flat to someone else.
9. Yesterday the boss fired Mr Barks.
10. Cologne Cathedral is an impressive building.
11. Hiking is less dangerous than mountaineering.

Exercise 45:
1. Bohnen; 2. Hütte; 3. Stiefel; 4. Kunst; 5. auf dem Boden; 6. Bande; 7. Quittung; 8. Meeresfrüchte; 9. Geschenk; 10. Krankenwagen; 11. Turnhalle; 12. Henkel; 13. Adler

Exercise 46:
1. He put on his hat and picked up his umbrella.
2. Hedgehogs are funny to look at; touching them is less funny.
3. There were many boats on the river.
4. Let's go! I don't like this kind of party.
5. Mr Bark's office is at the end of the corridor.
6. There were some haddocks in his net.
7. "Who put the poison in Mrs Hathaway's tea?" Holmes wondered.

8. The out-patient department was crowded so I had to wait for two hours.
9. Bees are very intelligent insects.
10. What's your recipe for this delicious cake?
11. The old man opened the door and put his suitcase in the hallway.
12. Our son attended a German secondary school.
13. Traffic in coffee has increased recently.

Exercise 47:
1. Hausaufgaben; 2. Biere; 3. Leichenbestatter, mitfühlend; 4. Vorlesung; 5. Landkarte; 6. Schlauch; 7. Kekse; 8. Hackfleisch; 9. Gebäude; 10. Nebel; 11. Lager; 12. Mord; 13. Foto

Exercise 48:
1. The murderer hid in a cave.
2. We keep our goods in a warehouse.
3. My son is the youngest entrepreneur in Germany.
4. "Now try to smile," the photographer said.
5. What did he recommend to you as reading material?
6. I prefer small boutiques to department stores.
7. The secretary put the form in a folder.
8. I can't wear these trousers. They're dirty.
9. His lack of education is shocking.
10. Did you help your mother with the housework?
11. Manure is a good fertilizer.
12. This cocktail is served with a mint leaf.
13. This is the best sponge-cake I've ever eaten!

Exercise 49:
1. der alte Hase; 2. Beförderung; 3. Kohle; 4. Aussicht; 5. Geschmack; 6. Fliege; 7. Landstreicher; 8. Schlange; 9. Geschwindigkeit/Tempo; 10. Bedeutungen; 11. Miete; 12. die Etikette; 13. Absender

Exercise 50:
1. My children never eat cabbage.
2. I don't rely on travel brochures.
3. How many keys does a piano have?
4. The snails have eaten my cabbage!
5. In my opinion Doctor Taylor is wrong.
6. I paid a lot of money for this vintage car.
7. I can't buy you this toy; my pension is too small.
8. What's in this bottle? There's no label on it.
9. Her parents were proud when she received her doctorate.
10. The radio station broadcast the President's speech.
11. I still haven't paid the monthly instalment for my car.
12. We picked up a hitch-hiker on our way to Detroit.
13. Our flight has been cancelled.

Exercise 51:
1. eine Kerze anzünden; 2. Ball; 3. ein freundliches Gesicht; 4. Rinde/Borke; 5. Zauber(-spruch); 6. Kartons; 7. Koffer; 8. einen schönen Blick auf Rom 9. auf der Bank; 10. ein klarer Fall; 11. genannt; 12. Spiel; 13. Blasen Sie die Kerze aus; 14. anwesend; 15. mögen; 16. ein Wettlauf mit der Zeit

Exercise 52:
1. Welche Art Obst/Welche Obstsorten; 2. leichte Musik; 3. Fall; 4. boxen; 5. Strafe; 6. bellen; 7. Wie buchstabiert/schreibt man dieses Wort; 8. Ball; 9. sieht ein bisschen aus wie; 10. räumte weg; 11. passen nicht zu; 12. versetzte ihm einen Schlag; 13. Geschenke; 14. am Ufer des Flusses; 15. die Menschheit (die menschliche Rasse); 16. rief sie die Polizei

Exercise 53:
1. Poor Roger was the only one without a partner at the ball.
2. I found a book of spells in our attic.
3. He carved her name in the bark.
4. I didn't pay the fine.
5. He put a box of matches in his pocket.
6. He won the race on a horse called "Lucky Star".
7. I don't like that kind of question.
8. The man sat down and lit a cigarette.
9. Holmes solved the case within two days.
10. The banks of the river were polluted with oil.
11. Everybody present applauded the speaker.
12. Blow the dust off this chair before you sit down.
13. Her hat and shoes matched wonderfully.

Exercise 54:
1. The teacher asked us to spell our names.
2. You'll clear the table, is that clear?
3. A girl like Alice is hard to convince.
4. When the postman rang, the dog began to bark.
5. The weather was fine, so they went for a walk.
6. I used to box as a teenager.
7. Mrs Turner called the children when it was time for dinner.
8. The two animals look different, but they belong to the same race.
9. Yesterday the bank was robbed.
10. Mr Turner bought a present for his wife.
11. The policeman was very kind and polite.
12. He had a light meal, then he went to bed.
13. The thief threw the dollar bills in a case.
14. The goalkeeper caught the ball with one hand.
15. Watson received a blow on his head.
16. The tennis match lasted four hours.

Exercise 55:
1a. *knew* – wusste; 1b. *new* – neu; 2a. *warn* – warnen; 2b. *worn* – getragen; 3a. *pain* – Schmerz; 3b. *pane* – (Fenster-) Scheibe; 4a. *threw* – warf; 4b. *through* – durch; 5a. *way* – Weg; 5b. *weigh* – wiegen; 6a. *forth* – her; 6b. *fourth* – vierte; 7a. *waist* – Taille; 7b. *waste* – Verschwendung

Exercise 56:
1a. *know* – kennen; 1b. *no* – nein/kein; 2a. *wear* – tragen; 2b. *where* – wo; 3a. *knows* – weiß; 3b. *nose* – Nase; 4a. *break* – zerbrechen; 4b. *brake* – bremsen; 5a. *fair* – fair/gerecht; 5b. *fare* – Fahrpreis; 6a. *ate* – aß; 6b. *eight* – acht; 7a. *wait* – warten; 7b. *weight* – Gewicht

Exercise 57:
1a. *cellar* – Keller; 1b. *seller* – Verkäufer; 2a. *dear* – lieb/teuer; 2b. *deer* – Rotwild/Hirsch; 3a. *weak* – schwach; 3b. *week* – Woche; 4a. *hear* – hören; 4b. *here* – hier; 5a. *saw* – sah; 5b. *sore* – entzündet/schmerzhaft; 6a. *pair* – Paar; 6b. *pear* – Birne; 7a. *too* – zu/auch; 7b. *two* – zwei; 7c. *to* – zu

Exercise 58:
1a. *hair* – Haare; 1b. *hare* – Hase; 2a. *peace* – Frieden; 2b. *piece* – Stück; 3a. *right* – richtig; 3b. *write* – schreiben; 4a. *role* – Rolle; 4b. *roll* – Brötchen; 5a. *heal* – heilen; 5b. *heel* – Absatz; 6a. *hole* – Loch; 6b. *whole* – ganze(-r, -s); 7a. *sail* – segeln; 7b. *sale* – Verkauf; 8a. *war* – Krieg; 8b. *wore* – trug

Exercise 59:
1a. *won* – gewonnen; 1b. *one* – eine(-r, -s); 2a. *knot* – Knoten; 2b. *not* – nicht; 3a. *meat* – Fleisch; 3b. *meet* – treffen; 4a. *steal* – stehlen; 4b. *steel* – Stahl; 5a. *their* – ihr; 5b. *they're* – sie sind; 5c. *there* – da; 6a. *pail* – Eimer; 6b. *pale* – blass; 7a. *read* – gelesen; 7b. *red* – rot

Exercise 60:
1a. *sauce* – Soße; 1b. *source* – Quelle; 2a. *Who's* – wer ist; 2b. *whose* – wessen; 3a. *higher* – höher; 3b. *hire* – mieten; 4a. *dessert* – Dessert; 4b. *desert* – verlassen; 5a. *weather* – Wetter; 5b. *whether* – ob; 6a. *passed* – bestanden; 6b. *past* – nach/vorbei; 7a. *son* – Sohn; 7b. *sun* – Sonne

Exercise 61:
1. <u>Where</u> are my glasses?
2. The mouse disappeared in a <u>hole</u>.
3. What's the <u>weather</u> like today?
4. "I've found a marble!" – "<u>Here's</u> another <u>one</u>!"
5. Our <u>new</u> sofa is very comfortable.
6. You can't bend the knife – it's made of <u>steel</u>.
7. I <u>know</u> she's <u>worn</u> that dress before.
8. I'm <u>not</u> interested in your offer.
9. <u>Aunt</u> Sylvie is my mother's sister.
10. We left the party at half past <u>eight</u>.
11. Do you <u>know</u> <u>where</u> he comes from?
12. The air was so cold that his <u>nose</u> turned red.
13. Her <u>pale</u> face turned red with embarrassment.
14. Three days had <u>passed</u> since the first crime.

Exercise 62:
1. After <u>two</u> <u>weeks</u> in prison the suspect confessed everything.
2. Did she put enough salt in the <u>sauce</u>?
3. My father was strict but <u>fair</u>.
4. <u>Who's</u> the most famous pop star?
5. I told you <u>to</u> paint the window frame, <u>not</u> the <u>pane</u>!
6. Are you trying <u>to</u> convince me?
7. I <u>saw</u> some wonderful paintings at the museum.
8. Who <u>threw</u> the stone at him?
9. You have no <u>right</u> to do that, Jesse.
10. If you <u>break</u> the law, you're a criminal.
11. What was your <u>role</u> in the play?
12. Is this beautiful vase for <u>sale</u>?
13. The chairs are <u>higher</u> than the table!
14. "<u>Where</u> are your parents?" – "<u>They're</u> at the theatre."

Exercise 63:
1. He was <u>too</u> <u>weak</u> <u>to</u> get up.
2. The <u>source</u> of the river has run dry.
3. He didn't have to pay the <u>fare</u> because he <u>knew</u> the driver.
4. Why don't you tell me <u>whose</u> car this is?
5. "This medicine will ease your <u>pain</u>," Doctor Taylor said.
6. You're <u>too</u> young to get married.
7. <u>One</u> <u>piece</u> of the jigsaw puzzle is missing!
8. My <u>son</u>'s name is Frederic.
9. His <u>sore</u> knee caused Mr Blair a lot of trouble.
10. The murderer came in <u>through</u> the kitchen window.
11. <u>Write</u> a composition on <u>one</u> of the following topics:
12. "Why don't you stop?" – "I can't find the <u>brake</u>!"
13. He bought three <u>rolls</u> for his ducks.

14. Do you <u>know</u> how to hoist a <u>sail</u>?
15. I <u>hired</u> a bicycle <u>to</u> get <u>to</u> the lake.
16. Why don't you <u>wear</u> your wedding ring?

Exercise 64:
1. Sorry? I didn't <u>hear</u> what you said.
2. "Why don't you tell me the <u>whole</u> story?" Holmes inquired.
3. He even <u>knew</u> my name!
4. That's the man who tried <u>to</u> <u>steal</u> my wallet!
5. They found a dead body down in the <u>cellar</u>.
6. In this play mother and daughter <u>desert</u> the father.
7. The <u>fourth</u> man in the room was Doctor Taylor.
8. <u>There's</u> a <u>hole</u> in the <u>heel</u> of <u>your</u> left sock.
9. We <u>meet</u> every day at the bus-stop.
10. My mother <u>won</u> the first prize in a beauty contest.
11. What colour is your <u>hair</u>?
12. <u>Two</u> hours later the doctor arrived.

Exercise 65:
1. Why didn't you <u>warn</u> them?
2. <u>There</u> was a <u>knot</u> in his fishing-line.
3. <u>There</u> <u>aren't</u> any eggs in the fridge.
4. Tracy <u>ate</u> some grapes for breakfast.
5. "He's a coward!" – "<u>No</u>, he isn't!"
6. "Mr Holmes <u>knows</u> everything," Watson explained <u>to</u> the concerned husband.
7. <u>There's</u> <u>no</u> water in the <u>pail</u>! Who has spilt it?
8. Put the verb in brackets into the <u>past</u>.
9. It's a quarter <u>past</u> five.
10. The <u>sun</u> is a star, <u>not</u> a planet.
11. <u>There</u> wasn't enough time to hide the gun.
12. How much <u>weight</u> did she lose in hospital?
13. I found a wallet on my <u>way</u> home.
14. He thinks that going to school is a <u>waste</u> of time.
15. He tried <u>to</u> cut the branch from the tree with a <u>saw</u>.
16. I'm going <u>to</u> the party, <u>whether</u> you like it or <u>not</u>.

Exercise 66:
1. The dog was running after the <u>hare</u>.
2. The book<u>seller</u> recommended this novel <u>to</u> me.
3. <u>There's</u> only <u>one</u> answer, Watson.
4. Mars was the Roman god of <u>war</u>.
5. The chef showed me how <u>to</u> slice the <u>meat</u> properly.
6. The wound won't <u>heal</u>, Doctor Taylor.
7. I <u>weigh</u> as much as our dog.
8. We talked about the <u>weather</u>, the future and so on and so <u>forth</u>.
9. He peeled the <u>pear</u> and cut it into quarters.
10. Would you like some cheese for <u>dessert</u>?
11. While hunting red <u>deer</u> they were attacked by a grizzly <u>bear</u>.
12. How many people lost <u>their</u> lives?
13. <u>Wait</u> for me, Roger!
14. Scarlett had a very narrow <u>waist</u>.
15. "Your <u>right</u> leg is broken, I'm afraid," Doctor Taylor said.

Exercise 67:
1a. drive; 1b. Riding; 2a. brought up; 2b. educate; 3a. learned; 3b. studied; 4a. do; 4b. makes; 5a. of 5b. let

Exercise 68:
1. Don't disturb your sister! She's studying in her room.
2. We rode in a car that had no air-conditioning.
3. "Let me see your leg," Doctor Taylor said.
4. Before I went to Spain, I had to learn Spanish.
5. Do you know how to make bread?
6. Mary was brought up by her grandmother.
7. My father drives an old car.
8. Leave the door open, it's too hot in here.
9. That is something I would never do.
10. My children were educated at a famous school.

Exercise 69:
1a. need; 1b. use; 2a. borrows; 2b. lent; 3a. watch; 3b. saw; 4a. deserves; 4b. earn; 5a. carried; 5b. wore

Exercise 70:
1. Nobody saw him running away.
2. My brother dreams of one day earning more than he can spend.
3. She lent me the best umbrella she had.
4. I have only used this toothbrush once.
5. He deserves the promotion, but some of his colleagues don't think so.
6. What else do you need, Roger?
7. He had forgotten his umbrella so he borrowed mine.
8. Holmes knew that someone was watching him.
9. The porter carried our luggage to the lift.

Exercise 71:
1a. got; 1b. stood; 2a. walk; 2b. go; 3a. heard; 3b. listened; 4a. remember; 4b. remind; 5a. brought; 5b. Take

Exercise 72:
1. Bring me my magnifying glass, Watson!
2. What time do the children get up?
3. This picture reminds me of my mother.
4. Roger stood up when the doctor entered.
5. Does he ever listen to the radio?
6. Are you going by bus or are you walking?
7. Mr Roberts decided to take his wife to the station.
8. My parents go to church every Sunday.
9. "How many shots did you hear that night?" Holmes asked.
10. She remembers giving him the car key.

Exercise 73:
1a. say; 1b. tell; 2a. attends; 2b. visited; 3a. see; 3b. looking; 4a. boil; 4b. cooking; 5a. ended; 5b. stopped

Exercise 74:
1. Why don't you say what you think?
2. Every evening Mrs Taylor cooks dinner for her family.
3. Judy's going to visit her uncle in London.
4. Have you seen that film before?
5. The film ends with a surprise.
6. Holmes looked out of the window.

7. I finally stopped smoking three weeks ago.
8. Tell me why you're laughing.
9. In our country all children over five must attend school.
10. Every morning my mother boils an egg for me.

Exercise 75:
1a. sky; 1b. heaven; 2a. jobs; 2b. work; 3a. road; 3b. streets; 4a. man; 4b. husbands; 5a. land; 5b. country

Exercise 76:
1. Did Mrs Grant find a job as a teacher in Birmingham?
2. The road to the village runs through a forest.
3. Uncle John owns a piece of land at the seaside.
4. At noon the sky cleared up again.
5. The secret of my success is hard work.
6. Who's the man with the long nose?
7. The Brownings live in a side-street behind the station.
8. On their honeymoon the young couple was in seventh heaven.
9. In many countries immigration is restricted by law.
10. The one with the long nose is my husband.

Exercise 77:
1a. shade; 1b. shadow; 2a. jam; 2b. marmalade; 3a. bottom; 3b. ground; 4a. woman; 4b. wife; 5a. Games; 5b. play

Exercise 78:
1. He's in love with the wife of another man.
2. You need ten oranges for two jars of marmalade?
3. The bottom of your fruit cake was a bit dry.
4. Stop following me, Watson! You're not my shadow, are you?
5. Our goalkeeper was penalized for foul play.
6. Alice sat on the ground and played with her doll.
7. This jam is made from apples.
8. The children were playing a ball game.
9. Put the ice cream in the shade, it's melting!
10. Who's the woman sitting next to him?

Exercise 79:
1a. colour; 1b. paint; 2a. life; 2b. living; 3a. price; 3b. prize; 4a. journey; 4b. Travel; 5a. company; 5b. societies

Exercise 80:
1. I prefer his company to being alone.
2. Last year they made a journey round the world.
3. The paint on the wall was still wet when Holmes arrived.
4. His film received a prize at that festival.
5. After five years he tired of living in a hotel.
6. My grandfather wrote a book about his travels.
7. A young woman lost her life in the accident.
8. Terrorism is a threat to society.
9. My favourite colour is blue.
10. Roger sold his car at a good price.

Exercise 81:
1a. flesh; 1b. meat; 2a. couple; 2b. pair; 3a. cause of; 3b. reasons for; 4a. during; 4b. While; 5a. as; 5b. like

Exercise 82:
1. This park is closed during the winter.
2. The cause of this fire is probably arson.
3. What kind of meat is in this soup?
4. Leave everything in this room as it is, Watson.
5. Our new neighbours are a young couple from Minnesota.
6. Don't answer the phone while I'm away.
7. The flesh of the yellow fruit tasted sweet.
8. My younger brother looks a bit like Huckleberry Finn.
9. What was his reason for saying that?
10. My mother bought three pairs of shoes at a sale at Harrods.

Exercise 83:
1a. finished; 1b. ready; 2a. difficult; 2b. bad; 3a. False; 3b. wrong; 4a. foreign; 4b. strange; 5a. little; 5b. small

Exercise 84:
1. This wardrobe is too small for my wife's clothes.
2. Nobody recognized Holmes because he wore a false beard.
3. I always feel uncomfortable in a strange town.
4. Mrs Taylor called the children as soon as dinner was ready.
5. It was difficult for me to understand the foreigner.
6. "Your suitcase is too heavy, sir," the man at the luggage counter said.
7. Tracy is such a sweet little child.
8. It's important to learn foreign languages at an early age.
9. Our new house is nearly finished.
10. She was so upset that she dialled the wrong number.

Exercise 85:
1. How is your husband, Mrs Taylor?
2. What time is it?
3. What about a coffee?
4. How was your trip to Italy?
5. What's Tracy's brother like?
6. What's the new teacher like?
7. What's the weather supposed to be like at the weekend?
8. How did you sleep on the new mattress?
9. How about going to the zoo?
10. How good is your German?
11. How do you spell the word "cuckoo"?
12. What was the concert like last night?

Exercise 86:
1. What's; 2. What; 3. How; 4. What; 5. What; 6. How; 7. What; 8. What; 9. How; 10. What; 11. What's; 12. How; 13. What

Exercise 87:
1. invited; 2. buy/stand; 3. treated; 4. invited/asked; 5. treated; 6. ask/invite; 7. stand/buy; 8. bought/stood; 9. stood; 10. buy/stand; 11. invited/asked

Exercise 88:
1. Who's speaking, please?
2. Pardon/Sorry? I didn't hear what you said.

3. "Would you like some tea?" – "Yes, please."
4. Two cups of coffee, please.
5. "It's late." – "Sorry/Pardon?" – "I said it's late."
6. "Thank you for feeding the dog." – "You're welcome."
7. Take a seat, please.
8. "A packet of cigarettes, please." – "Here you are."
9. May I please explain the situation?
10. "Will you have another cup of coffee?" – "Yes, please."
11. Put the paper on the table, please.
12. Sorry/Pardon? What did you say?
13. "He's a lawyer." – "Pardon me? What is his profession?"
14. "Here's the umbrella you forgot." – "Oh thank you very much." – "Not at all."
15. "Thank you for all your help." – "Don't mention it."
16. Could you please show me the way to the station?
17. Could I speak to the manager, please?
18. "Thank you for driving me to the party." – "My pleasure."

Exercise 89:
1. Sorry; 2. I'm sorry; 3. Excuse me; 4. I'm sorry; 5. Sorry; 6. Excuse me; 7. I beg your pardon; 8. Pardon; 9. Excuse me; 10. Pardon

Teil B

Test 1:
1. A.; 2. C.; 3. B.; 4. B.; 5. A./D.; 6. C.; 7. C.; 8. A.; 9. B.; 10. B.; 11. A.; 12. B.; 13. A.; 14. B.; 15. C.; 16. A.; 17. A.; 18. B.; 19. C.; 20. A.; 21. A.; 22. C.; 23. C.

Test 2:
1. B.; 2. A.; 3. A.; 4. C.; 5. B.; 6. B.; 7. B.; 8. C.; 9. B.; 10. B.; 11. C.; 12. D.

Test 3:
1. C.; 2. B.; 3. C.; 4. A.; 5. C.; 6. A.; 7. C.; 8. C.; 9. A.; 10. C.; 11. B.; 12. B.; 13. C.; 14. C.; 15. C.; 16. C.; 17. B.; 18. A.; 19. B.; 20. A.; 21. B.; 22. B.; 23. A.; 24. A.; 25. B.

Test 4:
1. C.; 2. B.; 3. A.; 4. A.; 5. A.; 6. B.; 7. A.; 8. D.; 9. C.; 10. C.; 11. B.; 12. B.; 13. C.; 14. B.; 15. D.; 16. A.; 17. B.; 18. B.; 19. C.; 20. A.; 21. B.; 22. A.; 23. C.; 24. E.; 25. A.

Test 5:
1. B.; 2. A.; 3. C.; 4. B./C.; 5. B.; 6. C.; 7. C.; 8. C.; 9. A.; 10. A./C.; 11. B.; 12. A.; 13. A.; 14. B.; 15. A./B.; 16. C.; 17. A.; 18. B.; 19. B.; 20. C.; 21. B.; 22. C.; 23. C.; 24. B.; 25. B.; 26. C. 27. B.

Test 6:
1. C.; 2. B.; 3. C.; 4. A.; 5. B.; 6. B.; 7. C.; 8. A.; 9. B.; 10. C.; 11. B.; 12. B.; 13. A.; 14. A.; 15. A.; 16. A.; 17. B.; 18. B.; 19. A.; 20. A.; 21. C.

Test 7:
1. studied – learnt/learned; 2. happy – lucky; 3. pane – pain; 4. onliest – only; 5. waisted – wasted; 6. become – get; 7. make – do; 8. eventually – actually; 9. while – during; 10. brought – took; 11. fabric – factory; 12. through – threw; 13. let – leave; 14. paint – colour; 15. went – walked; 16. watch – see; 17. boiled – cooked; 18. borrowed – lent; 19. drive – ride; 20. weigh – way; 21. clearer – more clearly; 22. your – you're; 23. some – any; 24. wive – wife; 25. good – well; 26. teached – taught

Test 8:
1. still – yet, yet – still; 2. on – in, land – country, land – country, live – life; 3. too – to, roll – role; 4. boiled – cooked, there – their; 5. during – while, wandering – wondering, weather – whether; 6. peace – piece, off – of; 7. homework – housework, ready – finished; 8. lands – countries, with – at; 9. go – walk, fair – fare; 10. mens – men, life – lives, childs – children; 11. if – when, price – prize; 12. man's – husband's, hairs – hair, are – is; 13. in – on, weak – week; 14. serie – series, in – on; 15. you're – your, fly – flight; 16. potatos – potatoes, prize – price; 17. kind – child, knive – knife; 18. boot – boat, winked – waved; 19. foreigner – stranger, gang – corridor; 20. to – too, week – weak; 21. tramp – hitch–hike, drove – went; 22. short – shorts, it – them, sail – sale; 23. many – much, fruits – fruit; 24. this – these, trouser – trousers, is – are, to – too; 25. play – match, life – live, in – on; 26. hasn't – haven't, murder – murderer; 27. cattles – cattle, geted – got; 28. any – some, piece – peace

Test 9:
1. brakes; 2. past; 3. wearing; 4. difficult; 5. department store; 6. meet; 7. sky; 8. paint; 9. shorter; 10. city; 11. job; 12. kind; 13. to; 14. lend; 15. on; 16. borrow; 17. big; 18. of; 19. shade; 20. road; 21. wife; 22. every; 23. doing; 24. company; 25. flesh; 26. lazy; 27. cabbage; 28. past; 29. broadcast; 30. brilliant; 31. wolves; 32. wrong; 33. sauce; 34. weak

Test 10:
1. carry, too heavy; 2. babies, leave, bath; 3. boss, if; 4. when, stops; 5. at, in; 6. son, in; 7. husband, earns; 8. a lot of, information; 9. If, vintage car; 10. do, homework; 11. where, born; 12. luggage, customs; 13. in, visit; 14. too, wear, kind, hat; 15. ground, waved; 16. hole, steel; 17. these, stairs; 18. knot, remind; 19. wore, pair; 20. kind, to; 21. green one

Test 11:
1. What do you usually do at the weekend?
2. Don't you think this skirt is a little too loose?
3. When war broke out, he left the country at once.
4. When they had seen the cathedral they visited the museum.
5. What's the weather been like during your holiday?
6. She visits a new country every year.
7. When you're ready I'll bring in the coffee.
8. Roger gets too much pocket money.
9. At night the mice came out of their holes.
10. Some of the players spent the day before the big match in the country.
11. Which trousers are we talking about, the red ones or the blue ones?
12. You needn't carry the puppy, it can walk very well.
13. Roger hitch-hiked to Venice last Easter.
14. My new job is much worse than I expected.
15. They didn't have any matches so they couldn't light a fire.
16. He was sent to prison because he refused to pay the fine.
17. It was difficult to read the map in the rain.
18. I haven't finished with the paper yet.
19. He has a lot of free time but I haven't got much.
20. He left the pub without paying for his beer.
21. Our neighbour says there will be no pears this year.

Test 12:
1. Ein Krankenwagen brachte die schwangere Frau ins Krankenhaus.
2. Sie befanden ihn für schuldig und schickten ihn ins Gefängnis.
3. Sie gab dem Hund ein paar von ihren Keksen.
4. Ich muss morgen zur Bank gehen.
5. Normalerweise boxen sie in der Turnhalle.
6. Sie gibt ihr ganzes Geld für Kleidung aus.
7. Roger ist nicht fähig, sich seinen Lebensunterhalt zu verdienen.
8. Gestern hielt der neue Lehrer einen Vortrag.
9. Es ist ein Glück, dass das Auto nicht beschädigt ist.
10. Eigentlich war Peter derjenige, der es getan hat.
11. Dein Vater ist ein sehr vernünftiger Mann.
12. Ich verpasste den Zug und kam folglich zu spät.
13. Mein neues Auto ist so schnell wie deines.
14. Der Apfel, den du mir gegeben hast, war faulig.
15. Sein rüdes Benehmen verärgerte meine Eltern.
16. Als Kind war Mary sehr gehemmt.
17. Er ist ein freundlicher Mann; er hilft mir immer bei der Gartenarbeit.
18. Er schrieb seinen Namen auf ein leeres Blatt Papier.
19. Es war ein schöner Tag, deshalb machten sie einen Spaziergang.
20. Die alte Dame bewahrte all ihre Ersparnisse in dieser Schachtel auf.

Test 13:
1. My son spends hours watching television.
2. Anthony worked hard at school so he got a good job when he left.
3. Holmes didn't take the threat seriously.
4. The photographer hadn't taken any pictures for years.
5. What was the concert like yesterday?
6. Sorry I'm late.
7. Pardon? I didn't hear that.
8. I won't let you watch TV until you've finished your supper.
9. Do you have to pay for it yourself?
10. Do you remember your first day at school, Jennifer?

11. He polished his shoes before he left.
12. Our neighbour has got a big dog.
13. Don't be so lazy! Get up and help your father!
14. It's not very tactful to laugh about his nose.
15. You're smoking again! You're not very consistent, are you?
16. I bought the current issue of "Newsweek".
17. I was happy when I saw Grandma again.
18. There's too much sugar in this punch.

Test 14:
1. Er warnte uns davor, auf dem Eis zu gehen.
2. „Ich wünschte, es würde regnen", sagte der Bauer.
3. Hast du dich für einen Kurs eingeschrieben?
4. Er wurde im Wald von einer Schlange gebissen.
5. Halten Sie es für besser, Kinder zu Hause zu erziehen (= unterrichten)?
6. Als sie die Schule verließ, wurde sie Obsthändlerin.
7. Es war sehr tapfer von dir, in das brennende Haus zurückzugehen.
8. Tom kann nicht so schnell laufen wie ich.
9. Bevor er den Vertrag unterschrieb, berechnete er die Kosten.
10. Wie ist der Name der Firma, von der du deinen Videorekorder gemietet hast?
11. Die zwei Schauspieler sprachen kaum/sagten fast gar nichts.
12. Ich frage mich, woher sie von seinem Unfall wussten.
13. Er schwamm ziemlich nahe am Ufer aus Angst vor der Strömung.
14. „Räum diesen Verhau auf, bevor du zum Angeln gehst!", rief seine Mutter.
15. Sobald er etwas Geld verdient hatte, gab er es beim Pferderennen aus.
16. Der Unfall geschah gerade, als ich meinen Sicherheitsgurt anlegte.
17. Er lud sie nicht zum Mittagessen ein, weil er sehr beschäftigt war.
18. Es würde Millionen kosten, die Kuppel zu erneuern.
19. Großvater zeigte uns, wie man ohne Streichhölzer ein Feuer entfacht.
20. Was tust du lieber, (bei einem Spiel) mitspielen oder zuschauen?

Test 15:
1. He was much kinder to his oldest son than he was to the others.
2. The children were playing in the street when their parents returned.
3. We were just flying over the desert when a storm broke.
4. Watson received a blow to the head and sank to the ground.
5. It's impossible for me to study at home.
6. Some of the group didn't know the way.
7. My wife was ill for a week, and during that week she ate nothing.
8. The teacher said, "You may leave when you've finished."
9. Do you think the train will be on time?
10. Would you look after my goldfish while I'm away?
11. When he arrived she was still cooking the meal.
12. I've got 200 bottles of Italian wine in my cellar.
13. You should eat less meat if you want to lose weight.
14. On Sundays Grandfather used to get up early and go hiking.
15. They couldn't afford to live in the city.
16. It is easier to speak Chinese than to write it.
17. She wasted a whole afternoon looking for the receipt.
18. She made a sponge cake for the garden party.
19. These apples look delicious! I'll take eight of the red ones.
20. In the end she found out what was wrong with the car.